Don't Smile at the Monkeys:
Seven Rules Women Need to Survive
and Thrive in the Corporate Jungle

by Jennifer Thomé

Digitally published and printed in the United States of America.

ISBN 978-1-4991-9687-0

Some people speak to animals.
Not many listen.
That's the problem.

– A.A. Milne

Acknowledgements

My endless gratitude goes to the people who helped shape, create and polish this book, as well as those who inspired my confidence and growth during my time in the corporate jungle.

Special thanks go to Julie, for her energy, enthusiasm and editing, Michelle for lighting my fire, Mary for her brilliant insights, Jelena for her honest feedback, and Katherine for her encouragement.

Preface

Even the most powerful women struggle in the corporate workplace. The women whose experiences and wisdom I share in this book have made it as executives and accomplished entrepreneurs, but it was their reluctance to speak publicly about their long, arduous climb to the top that led me to put pen to paper, hoping to empower aspiring professionals on a much larger scale than one-on-one mentoring or private events ever could.

This book was conceptualized years ago while I was working as a business journalist and had to beg and plead professional women to agree to be featured in my magazine. Many of them preferred to turn the limelight in another direction and would only speak at off- the-record events. I also noticed that many of them were reluctant to talk about the hard climb to the top, preferring to share success stories and ignore the challenges and piles of monkey doo they had faced along the way.

What's more, many women treat life, and success, in the corporate jungle like a zero sum game, creating an unnecessary and hurtful level of hostility between fellow females. Seared into my memory is one event where I asked a leader from a major IT company how she dealt with coworker aggression. Her response was simple and condescending: "you just have to deal with it. If you can't, you should get out." She might as well have told all the vulnerable women in the room to go grow a pair! I was mortified that vulnerability was treated with such disdain.

My parents are both psychologists and I've always enjoyed piecing together the puzzles of the mind, so I immersed myself in reading everything I could find about what's really happening in the workplace. The journey began in management studies, crossed through psychology, sociology, biology and ethology before ending up here: a comprehensive overview of what happens in the workplace on biological, psychological and emotional levels, coupled with advice on how to thrive in this complex environment.

Implementing the tools that I teach in this book may seem unnatural at times. Research by Pauline R. Clance and Suzanne A. Imes shows that women often suffer from Impostor Syndrome–the tendency to see themselves as being mistakenly over-valued by others, and that their success is a function of oversight or luck, rather than hard work and skill. In order to overcome this tendency, the book doesn't just offer keys to success (let's face it: if you don't feel entitled to success, you need more than just the keys!), but also a framework that will help you understand your feelings and actions–and those of others–and make the climb to the top seem natural and logical.

I'd read about many of the concepts in this book throughout my career, but it wasn't until I nearly perished at the hands of a Balinese monkey that I truly understood them. Long story short, I helped a parched monkey get a drink of water, and, pleased at this perfect moment of cross-species cooperation, I offered him a smile. To me, it was a friendly gesture. To him, it was a nasty threat.

Not surprisingly, the monkey attacked me and chased me out of the forest. It was then I truly understood how being a people pleaser had been misunderstood by my colleagues and detrimental to my career and self-esteem. Not only had I meddled in affairs that weren't mine, but I had also used the wrong signals to communicate with this and the other monkeys in my life. It was at that very moment that the title of this book was conceived.

This book covers a lot of ground, and it may force you to rethink who you are at work and in your life in the corporate jungle. Don't be daunted. Just keep following the river upstream, making small changes along the way and before you know it you'll finally feel like you've made it back to civilization. Trust me, once you get there and you look back on your journey, you'll be glad you took those first terrifying steps.

A Word about Monkeys

There will be many instances in this book where you'll find yourself thinking, "Oh! She's most certainly talking about men when she says 'monkeys!'" While that is often the case, it's not quite that simple. Both men and women can be monkeys, and the term refers to a specific group of people whose learned and natural tendencies seem to align perfectly with the needs and culture of the corporate jungle.

Monkeys are individualistic, determined, focused and competitive. They thrive naturally in the corporate jungle and have a real knack for identifying goals and reaching them that often eludes non-monkeys. However, when their natural strengths are exaggerated, they can come off as self-serving, selfish, ruthless and overzealous.

But as you'll learn, when you flip the mirror and take a good look at the non-monkeys in the jungle, you'll find the same dichotomy. The non-monkeys (that's us!) are strong and determined as well, but much more concerned with building welcoming inclusive environments and communities. We look at the overall health of a system rather than focusing on goals, and we excel at multitasking and seeing the greater picture. We're caring, careful and cooperative, but when these traits are exaggerated, we tend to lose ourselves and can come off as dallying, needy, overbearing and unfocused. The monkey sees these kinds of behaviors as an annoying waste of time, just as we see the monkey's actions as brash and demotivating.

As said, monkeys can be both male and female, and I've come across a fair number of both. When examining personality and professional patterns, biology supports a sex-based line between males and females, but the bottom line is simple: neither way of being is perfect or right. Their value lies in which perspective you have and how you put your talents to use for your own career and the greater good. Both have their merits and their faults, and both are dependent upon your point of view. The corporate jungle is overrun with monkeys and tends to favor them, so understanding how they operate and how to work with them is critical to your success.

Table of Contents

Rule # 1 Work Like an Animal

If you're going to thrive in the corporate jungle, you're going to have to be faster, smarter and more prepared than the other animals that share your habitat. That is what this book is all about. But before we get into the nitty-gritty of how to do this, you'll have to change your overall thinking toward your career, and learn to work (and live) like an animal.

Research supports that women are just as competitive as men, and that we've had our powerful survival instincts systematically bred out of us by a society that wants to keep us in our place.

While more and more companies have realized the benefits that feminine strengths contribute to the workplace–such as community building, non-zero sum thinking and better communications–there are still many areas in the corporate jungle where acting like a woman is not enough.

Fortunately, living like a monkey doesn't just mean learning "male" characteristics–it also means letting go of some of the more restrictive female traits that have been holding us back over the years, such as being demure, putting our needs behind those of others and not speaking our minds.

This chapter covers what you'll need to get you thinking like a monkey. Once you've got those down we'll be ready to launch into the real-life survival skills you'll need to become queen of the jungle.

In this chapter you will
• Learn how to succeed by putting your own needs first
• Develop deep, single-minded concentration and focus to help you achieve your goals
• Balance long-term planning against your immediate needs
• Recover from your mistakes and flourish after failures
• Get more work done by working less

Put Yourself First

This is the most basic rule of the jungle, but for many women, it's also the hardest to master. As women, we are both biologically predisposed and culturally programmed to put the needs of others before our own and take care of the pack.

While this behavior makes sense when we're living in small communities or taking care of our families, it doesn't make sense in the corporate jungle. Here our hard work isn't balanced with the equal contributions from other community members, and quickly becomes an Achilles heel that allows both the jungle and the monkeys to take advantage of us.

If the mere thought of putting yourself first makes you feel queasy, write this down and hang it somewhere where you can see it all the time: "Taking care of yourself is empowering to you and others. There is nothing wrong with taking care of yourself."

Neither life nor business are zero-sum games: both are bountiful, and if you're starving, that simply means that you haven't made yourself a priority. Chances are, you've put in the hours and energy, and ended up sharing your hard-won bananas with everyone along the way.

When you act selflessly, you're actually creating a jungle full of codependent creatures who rely on your easy and inexpensive services, thus undermining yourself, making it harder for other non-monkeys to learn the skills they need to get ahead, and preventing the monkeys from growing and learning how to do their own dirty work.

Putting yourself first is easier and more natural than you may think. On the most basic level, it means doing things that you actually want to be doing and which will allow you to thrive and get ahead, all while being paid a fair wage. It also means not wasting your time on frivolous projects that don't improve your salary or your career prospects—like baking treats and reorganizing the company server. And if you're OCD and can't keep away from the server, then it also means promoting your own work so that others know just how much you're contributing. Trust me, they won't figure it out on their own.

Unfortunately, looking out for yourself isn't the most popular option for women in the workplace. Research from Harvard and Carnegie Mellon Universities has suggested that women who ask for raises can be perceived as being demanding and less friendly, so it's wise to ask with a feminine touch. We'll talk about how to do this a little later in the book.

The reason that some bosses are taken aback when women ask for raises is because we have misled them to believe that we wouldn't. In the years that women have been in the corporate jungle, we have been happily taking the scraps for the good of the company, not realizing the abundance that was really out there. We've trained the monkeys to think that we are not really interested in walking away with the most delicious fruits. Understand that the company will do even better with well-paid and fully engaged employees, so by asking for a raise you're setting yourself and your company up for greater success.

But regardless of how you may come off to others, it's crucial that you demand the things that you need and deserve in your career. If you don't, you'll be at risk of committing the "Million Dollar Mistake," in which accepting a 1 percent standard raise instead of asking for a 4 percent annual raise means that you'll retire $1 million short of your earning potential.

Focus and Specialize

Our intrinsic habit of caring for the community has made women excellent multitaskers, both at work and at home. While this can be very useful, it sometimes leads to women being overlooked for their achievements and locked into certain positions because their bosses are unclear as to what their specialties are, or because those supervisors are unwilling to lose their best Janes-of-all-trades by moving them into other departments. Can you blame them?

But being stuck in a position and not doing anything about it is committing career suicide. Even if you're happy in your department and your position, you need to prove yourself and excel in order to get those golden promotions that will make sure that you don't end up a poor statistic in your retirement. Women live longer than men, but too many of us end up impoverished because we retire initially with less money in the bank and are then more likely run out because we live longer than our male counterparts.

So start by being really honest with yourself about the things that you need and want. The most basic thing you need is your salary to cover your living expenses. Add to that the things that you want: a great working environment, travel, time for family and money for all the things that make life worth living. Add up what it would take for you to live your dream life, sketch out what your dream job would look like and pursue your goal with single-minded focus!

One way to create greater focus, sharpen your mind and clear your thoughts is meditation. And even taking as little as two minutes a day to scan your body and release tension and visualize your goals can help keep you grounded and connected. It also makes your food taste more delicious, music sound better, sex more enjoyable and protects your brain against oxidative stress and mental illness, according to one University of Oregon study.

The ability to focus that we associate with meditation is one of the most common traits of successful people I witnessed in my career, and I saw it come to life firsthand one of my mentees. From the start, we focused on defining her brand, narrowing down her repertoire and creating a consistent body of work that she was sending into the world via her media platform.

A few months after we wrapped up our work together, we caught up and she filled me in on where her life had taken her. While she hadn't followed through on her goal to write every single day (mostly because she was out of commission with malaria for a week), people were so impressed with the clarity of her vision that she was being bombarded with offers from television producers, nonprofits and even a handful of dignitaries who wanted to work with her.

She spent the next year working on a number of projects overseas before landing a full-ride scholarship to her graduate school of choice in the United States.

And you know what the best part of this was? She did it all by doing less. Before we started working together, she was trying to be everything to everyone and had nothing but a muddled brand, a disengaged following and a stressful lifestyle to show for it. Once she got on track with her brand, she was able to accomplish more by doing less, and to present a clear professional narrative to others.

Mark Your Territory

Planning your career means marking your territory, which means being honest about the things that belong to you. You've got to draw a line and set boundaries.

Our instincts tell us that we should take care of the pack and spend our time and energy supporting the efforts of others. We share because we care, but that is very unwise in the jungle. The only time we should share is if doing so promises to advance our projects or our careers.

Doing everything for everyone also dilutes your identity and makes it harder for others to reward you for your efforts. Think about it: when was the last time someone was rewarded for doing one thing right, while you did 50 amazing things and were left out in the cold? It happens all the time, and it is much more likely to happen to women because they don't mark their own territory and promote themselves.

When you stop offering everything up for free or in exchange for short-lived gratitude, you'll notice that people respect you more, and with that greater respect you also gain greater earning potential.

Remember to Rest

Sleep is vitally important in maintaining a strong, beautifully well-functioning body and strong nerves, but periodic rest on a larger scale is also critical to your success in the corporate jungle.

Too many of us have been indoctrinated into the Protestant work ethic that teaches that when we leave, our work won't get done (or that it will be done poorly) and that everything will fall to pieces.

As much as this belief serves the bottom lines of big corporations, the truth about vacation time is that is accelerates your productivity, and also forces you to get organized and delegate, both of which empower the people around you and drive them to greater action.

What's more, vacations also relieve stress (if they don't, you're doing it wrong!) and fuel innovation. So take what Richard Branson calls "inspiration vacations." Breaking the routine gives your mind an opportunity to refocus and reassess what's going on at work, and will allow you to fully assimilate all of the information sitting in the back corners of your brain and create better strategies.

The perfect length of time for this kind of vacation is 10 to 14 days. Studies have shown that anything longer than that will make it difficult to return to the office, but that anything shorter will not provide your brain with the adequate rest it needs to reboot and unleash its full potential to synergize all of the knowledge you've acquired at work.

If you're really pressed or haven't earned your vacation days yet, research has shown that simply planning vacations can be a major stress reliever, even if you don't go on them. Nonetheless, dream big and aim for a real vacation. Later in this book, we'll talk about why time spent in the office is detrimental to your health, and then you'll fully understand why it's so critical to get out every once in a while.

Plan for Winter

No one knows for sure why women have a harder time putting their finances in order–maybe our parents never taught us, or perhaps our natural inclination to think communally means we spend little effort planning our own retirement and focus on the wellbeing of our family in the present–but the facts speak for themselves: women are more likely to end up poor, on food stamps, on the street and filing for bankruptcy.

We already know that part of this is caused by our unwillingness to ask for more, and our banana-headed monkey bosses's inability to realize that we are worth more. But blaming others very rarely brings about any real or lasting change, and if you want to thrive in your retirement, you'll have to learn to do your own planning.

The first step is to create a career plan that ensures long-term growth, both in your finances and your skill sets. There are numerous resources you can turn to, but one of the best ways to plan your career is learn about people who you sincerely admire and aspire to be like. Most people enjoy the attention and will happily share their stories with you.

I have heard some anecdotal evidence about higher-ranking women undermining young women in the workforce because the space for women at the top is limited, but rest assured that those instances are rare, and when they happen, you should just keep looking for someone else. You don't want to spend your energy talking to saboteurs.

Once you have your career goal in place, make sure that all of the elements in your life are pointing in that direction. Learn the right skills, meet the right people, work on the right projects and get into the right circles. You'll learn many tips on how to do all of these things throughout this book.

Many people say that once you resolve to do something, the universe will conspire to help you. While I can't say that I know what the universe thinks, I do know this: humans are inherently helpful and love to see others thrive, so if you know what you want and can share that goal with them in a clear, concise manner, the jungle will align with and support you. The only reason it hasn't supported you thus far is that you've been too vague about what you really want or too afraid to seize it.

Since your life plan includes what will happen once you escape the corporate jungle, make sure that you put aside money and invest in a way that makes sense to you. All too often women focus on the near-term because it's tangible and easy, and because we've been told that someone else will look out for us.

Thinking about investing is often counterintuitive to women because we've been taught that we're risk adverse and bad at math (both of those are false, by the way), and that someone else will take care of it. The truth is, however, that men die earlier than women and many relationships fall apart, so make sure that you're actively planning your own retirement and investments, learn from your mistakes, acquire new skills and fall in love with the game.

Stay in the Here and Now

Because women have traditionally been closely tied to the pack and were in charge of protecting the weakest members, our instincts are hard-wired to look for problems and patterns in everything to ensure that we avoid or quickly resolve the same threat the next time it comes around so that we can quickly resolve the threat the next time it comes around.

This is why our brains more readily imprint stressful and negative situations to facilitate a quick recall of what happened. This creates anxiety and worry, both of which were born as these are survival mechanisms but that have proven themselves to be a menace to our modern minds as they make it so much harder to overcome stressful situations and break worry habits.

Picture this: something goes wrong at work. Your first reaction is to stress about it, mull about it and then to resolve it. Even though you've found a solution to the problem, your brain has imprinted the formula "problem + stress + mulling = solution" into your memory bank, meaning that every time you run into a similar problem, your brain will recall the same pattern. That's why it's so hard to break out of the stress cycle.

When it comes to workplace challenges, our monkey counterparts have a distinct advantage over us: they tend to look for immediate solutions and aren't plagued by guilt or over-examination of the situation. When they run into a problem, monkeys spend less time agonizing about its effects and consequences, and immediately jump into problem solving mode. Therefore, their memory bank imprint is: "problem + problem solving = solution."

This keeps monkeys in the moment, leaves them open to opportunities and allows them to react to situations in real time. The added benefit of being so focused on the here-and-now is that they waste little time on guilt, which is perhaps one of the biggest drains on time and energy there is.

Unfortunately, there is no easy way to train your brain to forget these deeply ingrained stress patterns other than practice. In chapters ahead, you'll soon learn tools you can use to change your reactions and reprogram your brain.

If you really want to thrive in the corporate jungle you'll have to let go of guilt. You have to accept that life, by its very nature, is faulty. Our goal as human beings is to grow and evolve, and that means walking away from our mistakes with our chins held high and the determination to learn from the experience.

I worked with a publishing executive who is the master of the present moment. Her career began abruptly when she was an office manager and the company was raided for an audit because a competitor had accused them of illegal operations. Now, living in a country where she knew that you're guilty until proven innocent and that they'd likely never get their equipment back, she immediately grabbed her boss's computer and files, climbed onto the ledge of the building and hid them on top of the AC unit. Her boss, needless to say, was extremely impressed with her clever and swift action. They actually ended up becoming business partners and life partners.

Out of all the people I've ever worked with, I've never seen anyone so keenly aware of her surroundings: instead of worrying about the drama, gossip and small things that were happening in the office and the market, she kept an eye open for greater trends, and as such, was always the first to know of—and take full advantage of–sudden changes in the market. She was hardly ever caught off guard and never sentimental about having to kill a product that didn't work. She always seemed to be a couple of steps ahead of her competition.

The Jungle Knows No Failure

Have you ever walked away from something feeling like a failure? Of course you have! We all have, and that's only human. But there is something that the animals know which allows them to thrive while we are stuck just trying to survive: the jungle knows no failure.

There is one exception to that rule, and that is death. Everything else is an opportunity to learn, and frankly, most of the time you spend dwelling on things is time wasted. Others have long since forgotten what happened, and you have wasted many precious opportunities to do better and prove yourself by mulling over your mistakes or worrying what might happen. The more time we waste worrying about what bad things did or may happen, the less time we have to make amazing things happen.

Monkeys see failure as part of the learning process, and instead of dwelling on what went wrong, they immediately go into salvage mode and do whatever it takes to fix it and move on. This is not only a much more productive way to handle failures, but it also creates a positive feedback loop that turns a negative experience into a positive one. If you start rewarding yourself for all the tiny mistakes you've fixed, you'll soon lose your fear of failure.

That being said, you'll want to be very careful with how you handle "failures" in the office. Because we are communal creatures, our instincts tell us to talk it through, work it out and apologize. Don't do any of those! If you go to a monkey and dwell on the details of your failure, you are taking ownership of the problem rather than the solution. Instead, acknowledge that something didn't work, don't apologize and immediately start working on a solution.

With society and business changing faster than we could have ever imagined, one of the most common traits that modern employers seek in their employees is grit–the ability to stick to a project and fight your way through to the end, regardless of setbacks. So the next time you're worried about making a mistake, take a deep breath and throw yourself in headfirst. You will come out stronger, more confident and more attractive to your monkey colleagues and bosses.

The one thing I've always loved about interviewing serial entrepreneurs is this very attitude toward failure. While most of us spend our days in fear of messing up, these brave business people embrace their mistakes, squeeze every last inch of wisdom out of the situation, do some damage control and then move on to bigger and better things.

One entrepreneur I interviewed had a handful of sunken businesses behind him, but with the way he talked about them, you'd never know that his failures had been anything but spectacular learning experiences. When he talked about what had happened to those companies, he never spent time dwelling on what had gone wrong or what he could have done better. No, he spent every breath related to his past failures talking about how much he'd learned, grown and gotten out of them.

The effect? When people saw how much he learned from of his failures (which really didn't look like failures at all because of his great attitude), they couldn't help but want to be associated with him, and through their continued support and funding he was able to open a chain restaurant that was unstoppable. His past experiences and his attitude toward failure had made him bulletproof, and because he knew all the ways to mess up, he created a company that was as close to flawless as I have ever seen.

Another way to think about this is a great tradition called "My Greatest Failure." I once hosted an event where a number of senior women executives gathered to share their greatest failures and what they had learned as a consequence thereof. The event was amazing. In a room full of perfectionists, these women opened up and talked about the many mistakes they had made in their careers, and, much like the serial entrepreneur, shared what they had learned and how these experiences had made them stronger.

While you may be accustomed to being at the head of the pack, don't let your comfort with excellence in a certain area of life derail your professional growth. Carol Dweck, author of *Mindset: The New Psychology of Success*, puts it well when she says that it takes time for potential to flower. Give yourself that time, and don't be intimidated by the possibility of failure. Remember, you were hired for your capabilities and your personality: why not go out on a limb so you can show them just how much you can really accomplish?

Keep Growing

Verne Harnish, the author of the *Rockefeller Habits* and the founder of the Entrepreneur's Organization, loves to start his talks with the following story:

> *Every morning in Africa, a gazelle wakes up. It knows it must run faster than the fastest lion or it will be killed... Every morning a lion wakes up. It knows it must outrun the slowest gazelle or it will starve to death. It doesn't matter whether you are a lion or a gazelle...when the sun comes up you'd better be running.*

There are very few jobs out there that will remain unchanged during our lifetimes, and where loyalty without growth will be rewarded.

The corporate jungle is a vast and complex system filled with dangers and challenges, and there are always new threats emerging, both natural and man-made. If your sole goal is to survive, keep moving the way you are now. But if you want to thrive and claim your spot as queen of the jungle, you're going to have to overcome your natural tendencies and habits to become faster, smarter and stronger than the creatures around you.

Recap: Work Like an Animal

Always Put Yourself First
Stop feeling guilty about investing more energy in yourself than others, right now. It's not your job and it's not your responsibility to take care of them. Realize that the corporate jungle is a bountiful workplace and claim your rightful piece of the resources. Don't let your work control your life, and always remember that if you openly pursue your passions, the jungle will align itself with you and support you with whatever you need.

Live in the Present
Don't waste your energy worrying about the past or the future. Instead, invest your energy in living every minute to the fullest and preparing for a better tomorrow. Worry and guilt are negative energies that rob you of your vital essence. But hope, aspirations and productivity will restore that energy.

Develop Determination and Focus
Stop letting yourself be distracted by things that aren't contributing to your career success. Once you stop wasting your time, you'll free your mind to enjoy life and think about more important matters. Finish each of your projects with single-minded dedication and make sure that all of your actions align with your life's goals.

Balance Needs with Long-Term Plans

It's hard to keep an eye on everything, but taking the time to have a long-term strategy and retirement plan will help align your work, will give meaning to the daily grind and will help keep the minor aggravations in perspective.

Boost Your Productivity with Vacations

Giving your body and mind periodic will not only help you recover on a physical and psychological level, but will also allow you to gain a greater perspective and generate new ideas to improve your workflow. Use all of your vacation days because you've earned them. Avoid staying late at the office. It makes you look like you can't finish your work.

Keep Evolving

The jungle may be bountiful, and while there are always enough resources, there will also be a number of animals waiting to take them from you.

Rule # 2 Unleash your Inner Beast

Life in the corporate jungle is full of surprises—some good, some bad, and some downright nasty. Perhaps one of the most shocking things you'll find is that being friendly and other virtuous attitudes and actions are no longer an asset and can actually land you in piranha-infested waters. The problem is that people in the jungle are wired differently, and unless you learn to understand things from their perspective, you will spend the next four decades scratching your head trying to figure out exactly what you've done wrong again this time.

In this chapter, you'll

• Figure out why being nice doesn't get you anywhere
• Find out what really causes workplace conflict, and what you can do to avoid it
• Discover the differences between the male and female brain and how they can affect your work life
• Learn the strengths of the female brain and how to leverage them at work
• Plus, you'll find out the shocking truth about the real cost of being underpaid and underappreciated in the workplace

Don't Smile at the Monkeys

You know how people always tell you that you'll catch more flies with honey? It's true, of course, but why on earth would you want to catch more flies? Wouldn't it be easier to ignore them? Or get an electric zapper?

Many women make the mistake of being excessively nice in the office–and yes, our biology is to blame–but being nice sends a strong signal that you are always willing to support others and that you're easy to manipulate because you're so agreeable. It also sends the message that you want to serve, even if it is as a doormat. Before you know it, you'll simply become an assistant, or even worse, a pawn in someone's game. Being excessively nice sends a clear message that people do not have to show you respect to earn your appreciation because you'll give it to them regardless.

Even worse, your colleagues may become suspicious because acting nicely is something that is foreign to them, or that they only employ when they are trying to get something. If that is the case, your niceness may actually backfire and cause them to think that you're sucking up or trying to manipulate them.

So instead of being nice, try being a little apathetic. Not indifferent to your job, of course, but to people–truth be told, anyone else equally qualified could be doing those jobs and filling those seats, so unless your colleagues prove themselves, you have no reason to show them any appreciation. This sets the bar in very straightforward way and immediately raises your credibility because you don't appear to think that everything is good without scrutinizing it. Not only

37

that, but your coolness also gives you much more leverage to crack down on things when they aren't going well.

Conversely, don't take it personally when people don't like you instantaneously. The truth is, it's not their job to like you, only to work with you, and as the new person you pose a threat to them. It's hard and counterintuitive, but think of it this way: the respect that you earn is worth a lot more than that which was simply given to you.

I once worked with a professional consultant who taught me everything I know about conducting a hiring interview. Like so many other women, I'd mastered the art of pleasantries and could really work a conversation. I was known as one of the best journalists in my field, not because I was the best writer, but because people liked talking to me and trusted me, and were always happy to introduce me to their friends because of how well I'd brought their stories to life. In short: I always got the best scoop.

Well, my skills in charming people became relatively useless when I was thrown into HR for a few months while they recruited a new manager. Sure, I was able to put out fires, but all too often the ashes kept on smoldering because I wasn't tough enough to get to the bottom of things. When the trainer came on board, she taught me the art of controlling the conversation and sending the right message.

The first lesson was never to make people feel too welcome. Once you do, it's too easy to become distracted by chitchat, and what's more, you're feeding them positive energy which will changes the outcome of the interview. You should also never make people feel unwelcome. The key is to be neutral.

Once you get to know people on these neutral terms, your kindness can actually bring about much more powerful goals than if you'd been nice all along. By bringing out your kind side during specific parts of the conversation you are rewarding the other person for what they've just done, and in turn, encouraging them to share even more details with you. It's the most effective way to get honest responses, gauge how a person works in a neutral environment and reward their honesty, which will allow you to dig deeper.

The Root of Bullying

How often has this happened to you? You're at work, doing the best you possibly can while also making sure that others are getting the attention, respect and support they need. Then, out of nowhere, you're blindsided by an aggressive colleague, an office bully, a condescending manager, or someone who just seems to have woken up on the wrong side of the jungle.

Perplexed, you start blaming yourself. Perhaps you said something wrong, or stepped on someone's toes? Maybe you stole the limelight from someone without realizing it? You go over every conversation, interaction and email with a fine-toothed comb, trying to find the source of the conflict. You can feel it in your gut: you obviously did something wrong and that is why they are mad at you.

Well, the truth is, you did do something wrong: you did a good job. The sad truth of the corporate jungle is that many of its inhabitants see it has having limited resources, or what politicians call a zero-sum game. That means that at the end of the day, there is only so much to go around, and your proactive, positive and likable self poses an inherent threat to their banana stash. And so they lash out.

To make things better, you reach out to them and offer a peace papaya, along with a big smile. You go out of their way to make them feel more comfortable and appreciated. You even step out of the spotlight and downplay your accomplishments, all in hopes of amending the relationship. Before you know it, you're in a closed meeting with supervisors where your colleague blurts out how they hate working with you because you're entitled, snobby and think you're better than everyone else. And all you can think is: "Huh?"

This happened to me many years ago in my first real job, and then again in my second, and yet again in my third. I never quite figured out what I had done wrong until I began working with a consultant who noted that I must really tick people off by being so enamored with my work. As I shared my story, she quickly informed me that there was a number of things I had done wrong over the years, but that my greatest crime was this: I let them get away with it.

From my perspective, I had done everything right: I had been helpful, smart, engaged and charming to boot. What I didn't realize is that I posed a huge threat to my colleagues. In my mind, they were my seniors and I respected them, but they knew that if they had been in my role, they would have seized any chance to grab the better role and run for it. To them, the workplace isn't a community that mutually supports one another for the greater good; it's a place where you prove that you are the best in order to move the top as soon as possible.

Once my colleagues were injured, I committed the second mistake: I chased them. When my colleagues lashed out they were trying to push me down and away–by turning on the charm offensive I essentially engaged in the pursuit, not only stepping up my game in order to make sure I was doing a good job, but also throwing it in their face by extra pleasant and extra helpful. All they wanted was to push me into their shadow, and into submission.

The more I opened up about my experience with office bullies the more I heard the same stories from other women: bullying is incredibly common, but despite all the awareness that has come about on the topic in the past few years, bosses are still reluctant to fire or reprimand them.

Bullies, it turns out, are often appreciated by higher ups for their loyalty and their ability to herd the office sheep, if you will. The whistleblowers, on the other hand, often get written off as a tattletale and a complainer, thus lowering their opinion of you and therefore your chances of getting promoted.

The only way to defeat a bully is to avoid them if they are circling and bite back once they attack. This is how I dealt with my last bully. I made a habit of staying cool, avoiding meetings that would give him the opportunity to lash out, ignoring his negative comments, and biting back when attacked. Showing my teeth–and that I wasn't perfect–reassured him and actually convinced him that we were on the same level.

He never gave me a problem again.

Bullies come in all shapes and sizes, and there is no shortage of female bullies. From the many stories I've heard, though, the overwhelming bully-bullee dynamic is male versus female, and while it's easy to attest these differences to culture, there are also a number of neurological and communications problems that might be exasperating the situation. Our biology is often a big driver of the conflicts and micro-conflicts we experience.

Most of us were raised with the idea that we should treat others the way we want to be treated, but the logical fallacy of this notion is that by doing so we are ignoring how others might actually *want* to be treated. In the case of bullies, this often means that they want you to defer to them or at least put up a fight. Treating them with grace and kindness and trying to make them happy actually strikes them as suspicious and passive aggressive.

Women are adept at perceiving and empathizing with other creatures, which is why it's so hard for us to understand when others do not share our feelings or have any desire to do so. While cultural factors weigh heavily in workplace altercations, our biology is a big driver of the conflicts and micro-conflicts we experience.

You must always remember that everyone is wired differently. Each person has their own motivations, their own history, their own lenses for viewing the world, their own problems, their own egos, and consequently, they interpret every situation differently than you do.

Luckily there are distinct patterns that can help you make sense of others' behavior, which we'll talk about in this chapter before moving on to how you can use your understanding of biology and psychology to make the workplace work for you, rather than against you.

A few years back I found myself a private dinner with the head of marketing of a Fortune 500 company. She was sharing her thoughts on storytelling, and I couldn't help but be taken aback by her candid approach to talking about the differences between the sexes as she made the following point: marketing is brutally honest about the fact that there are differences between women and men. Different things excite us and advertising to the sexes is a real science, and yet we tiptoe around the fact that there is a difference between women and men in the political aspects of our lives.

Alexia Parks, the author of *Hardwired: The 10 Major Traits of Women Hardwired by Evolution That Can Save the World* also tackles this subject head-on in her short but informative book. In it, she argues that the more feminine characteristics of being inclusive and having a wider sense of perception are exactly what are needed by the leaders of today to help them deal with an increasingly complex world.

Another author to tackle this subject is John Gerzema, author of *The Athena Doctrine*, who traveled the world interviewing men and women business leaders who led their companies using "feminine" leadership qualities such as nurturing, listening, collaborating and sharing to solve problems, increase profits and redefine success.

The Differences between Women and Men

Let's start with differences between women and men. Women and men are different in so many ways, and most of them are top-down differences in the brain that not only change the way we look and act, but also how we perceive things and react to them.

Here are some basic physical differences in the brain and their fascinating impacts on our working lives:

Most Men Are Left-Brain Dominant
This makes them more task-oriented and less communicative than their right-left balanced female counterparts. Keep this in mind when talking to men about work projects: they will likely be a lot less interested in the details than they are in reaching their goal.

Women Have More Balanced Brains
This explains why we are generally better at bridging different ways of working and thinking. It is also cited as a cause for our better communication skills and emotional intelligence. Most men, on the other hand, have trouble picking up on emotional cues, so it's critical to be direct and not rely on subtle cues to get your message across.

We See the World Differently
Men excel at spatial visualization—like rotating objects in their minds—and across cultures are better at judging angles and navigating by cardinal directions. That being said, women, with our chubby parietal region,

tend to see more color and detail, which gives us the advantage when it comes to remembering objects and where they have been placed.

Men Might Be Better at Math
Men have a larger inferior-parietal lobe, which has been attributed to better math skills. But don't let that stop you! Scientists have found that in gender-equal societies, this difference actually vanishes.

Women Are Better at Language
Both areas of the brain that deal with language are larger in women, and on top of that, we also tend to use both halves of the brain to process language, giving us a big advantage in communications. Or does it? Sadly, your nuanced communications sometimes go straight over the heads of your male colleagues, so remember to keep your audience in mind when speaking.

Women Are More Emotional
Blame it on our well-endowed deep limbic system but we are more sensitive to emotions, more empathetic and more prone to depression. Couple that with our excellent language abilities and our drive to communicate, and it is no wonder that men perceive us as overly emotional.

We Handle Stress Differently
Evolutionarily speaking, women tended to the pack while men went out to hunt, which might explain why, when we're faced with stress, women "tend and befriend," and men "fight or flight." How does this

manifest? Women statistically prefer to talk through problems, take care of all affected people and seek compromise, while men will go in for the kill or withdraw. Keep this in mind the next time you're sharing with a monkey or pressing him to share with you.

Men Have Bigger Brains
Men's brains are 10% bigger than women's, as a matter of fact, but they aren't smarter. The added size is only there to support their additional body and muscle mass.

Now, does all of this really make a difference? Should you walk away with an inflated sense of self-worth, a deflated sense of possibility or the smug justification that all of your past corporate clashes are warranted? Absolutely not! The one thing you need to take away from this is that there are slight, neurological differences that influence our perception of the world–and that you should tune into them and leverage them in order to gain maximum success in the corporate jungle while also guarding yourself against the pitfalls of your own biology.

Think about it. When we first bid adieu to our monkey cousins, our lives were relatively simple. Men, who were endowed with greater physical strength, worked in teams to hunt. Everything that makes their brains special–from their spatial ability to their iron focus–enabled them to be better hunters.

Women, on the other hand, worked in groups to care for the family and gather sustenance–our attention to detail, attuned nature and ability to see color are critical survival traits.

While these traits are no longer necessary to our survival, the modern workplace–which evolved around the strengths and weaknesses of the monkeys–is an incredibly complex place, so being armed with this knowledge will allow you to stay ahead of the game and plan your moves accordingly. When you combine your natural talents with an understanding of the jungle and how it works, your feminine tendencies can be the most important weapons in your career arsenal.

What's Wrong with Working Like a Woman?

The pitfall of our biological inclinations to care for our community is that we often invest more of our energy into office relationships and our work than we should, thus draining our finite energy resources to the detriment of our personal lives. Furthermore, we often put the needs of the company before our own, which translates directly into less money, less satisfaction and poorer health. Here are some of the pitfalls of being a (statistically average) woman in the corporate jungle.

Lower Status is Bad for Your Health
Studies have shown that success and higher status boost your immune system, making you less likely to get sick and allowing you to recover more quickly from injury. People at the top are also a lot less likely to suffer from heart disease and bronchitis than underlings.

Lower Status is Depressing
A number of studies have shown the link between status, respect, your socioeconomic level and

depression. People higher up on the food chain are less likely to suffer depression, and when they do, they recover from it more quickly. In short, by not receiving your dues, you are more likely to suffer both disease and its physical consequences (such as increased rates of heart disease, the number one cause of death for many populations), but are also less likely to recover. Given that women already suffer from higher rates of depression than men, this issue deserves our attention.

Equal Work Does Not Earn Equal Pay

To this day, women still earn around 80 cents for every dollar that men earn, and that disparity is even greater for non-Caucasians. That doesn't even account for women who take time off to raise children, tend to ill parents and take part in other tasks commonly reserved for women.

Women Die Poor

While women earn less during their working years, few save enough or realize that Social Security benefits are calculated based on an average of your highest earning years, so you'll also earn less than your average male counterpart after you retire—no matter how long you worked. Add to that the fact that most women live longer than men, and you can see how this math does not work in our favor.

So you see, the implications of your actions and gender bias in the workplace reach far beyond the cubicle and might even follow you to your grave. If you need any inspiration whatsoever to climb up into that palm tree, figure out the lay of the land and start ruling the jungle, this list should be your battle cry.

The Perception Gap

Many men are befuddled by women's ceaseless ability to mull over seemingly identical options, while women are endlessly frustrated by their boss's or partner's inability to care about the details. This is a classic example of the Perception Gap, the space between what the two genders can perceive and care about. In other words, it's highly likely that those issues you thought were being ignored just never made it into the monkey's mind.

In the chart below you'll find common professional traits and how they are perceived in the workplace:

Traits	What He Sees	What She Sees
Attentive	Adoring, needy, neurotic	Excellent work ethic
Organized	Overly concerned	Very efficient
Overly Helpful	Trying to prove something, currying favor	Just trying to help
Focused	Concentrated	Not caring, self-absorbed
Driven	Tenacious	Apathetic, not caring, selfish
Caring	Needy, emasculating	Friendly, responsive
Short	Efficient	Rude
Elaborate	Trying to prove something, wasting time	Trying to share point of view

Flexible	Indecisive (when talked about), adaptive (when seen in action)	Adaptive, in-tune, concerned with company "well-being"
Collaborative	Needy, helpless, overbearing	Team player, respectful

The next time you're frustrated with a monkey, make a list of all the things you find obnoxious about him, and then put a positive spin on each of those items. Once you do, the traces of evolution will light up before your eyes, and you'll see that so many of the traits we find irritating rub us the wrong way simply because they aren't in line with our own thinking. Be sure to complete this exercise for yourself as well, but in reverse. You may be amazed at what you find, and pleasantly surprised at how many office clashes you'll be able to prevent.

In my interviews and research, I've found that the single biggest misunderstanding between men and women in the office is the perception of the purpose: generally speaking, men focus on the big goals, while women weave the maintenance of the office and its relationships into their path toward the bigger goal. From the male perspective, this looks like dilly-dallying, while from the female perspective, the male leaders are being unnecessarily curt and apathetic.

But before you run off changing your whole professional work life, keep in mind that this is a spectrum. Being a man does not automatically mean that you're bad at languages, just as being a woman does not disqualify you from a career in finance.

Again, these are just natural predispositions.

What you make of them, and your career, is entirely up to you. If you develop great skills and integrate them with your talents, you will be poised to become more powerful than all the other creatures in the jungle–a true force to be reckoned with.

Develop a Gut

Some of the most under appreciated allies we have in the corporate jungle are our instincts. Men are often hailed as having better "gut instincts," while women are called "intuitive." Both of these perceptions are actually two sides of the same coin.

Men, whose brains make them more inclined to focus on goals and achievements, appear to have better gut instincts when it comes to business. Women, on the other hand, have a natural knack for reading situations and people, two factors which are related to intuition. The two are essentially a varying expression of the same ability to hone in on subtle cues, but are applied to different aspects of office life.

To develop a better gut instinct you simply have to refocus your energy from relationships to your business goals. Once you immerse yourself in them, you will notice the same patterns and opportunities that men see when their gut instinct tells them to pay attention to something.

The real challenge will come when you start breaking the habit of second-guessing yourself, and the only way you can do this is by practice.

You Don't Need Balls to Be a Risk-Taker

It's no secret that women are seen as less competitive and less willing to take risks, which are often the excuses used to bar us from working in certain industries or serving as leaders. These notions are both outdated and biologically incorrect.

In the chapters ahead, you'll begin to discover that this perception is largely rooted in the way we act and communicate in the office, and that with a few changes, we can become strong competitors to our male counterparts. Don't worry—you can do so without being perceived as bossy or bitchy, a natural confusion that occurs when women start acting the way men do.

But let's get back to risk aversion. Certainly, women have instincts to protect their families, and if you look around, it seems pretty obvious that women are more likely than men to consider the needs of the team before making any big decisions. As noble as their intentions are, this can give the impression that women are stalling and therefore risk adverse. But is there a biological root for risk aversion in females?

Apparently not. A team of researchers studied competition and risk aversion in two different societies, the very patriarchal Masai and the very matriarchal Khasi. Women in the matriarchal society were more likely to engage in high-stakes gambling than men in a patriarchal society. That means taking risk is in our bones: we just need to re-train ourselves to do so.

That being said, women are more perceptive of minute facial movements and other biological indicators, so if your gut is telling you something is "off" about a person, don't write that feeling off. Dig deeper and you'll be happy that you did.

Recap: Don't Smile at the Monkeys

The Workplace Evolved around the Monkeys

Don't ever feel bad about the fact that thriving in the workplace seems hard, unnatural or frustrating. The simple truth is that the workplace evolved around the monkeys, and the fact that you're surviving at all is a great start. Now you just have to learn how to run with the animals and outsmart them to get ahead of the game.

Look at Things from the Jungle's Perspective

To you, the workplace should probably be a place where people work together for the greater good of the community–but that's not what the monkeys think. Before taking any action, be sure to put on your jungle-colored glasses to make sure you're thinking like a monkey and doing the right thing for the situation.

Understand Your Inherent Strengths and Their Inborn Weaknesses

Not everyone is created equally but everyone has an innate set of strengths that they can engage to get the most out of their careers. Combine that with your understanding of the monkey mind and you can write your own ticket. As Sun Tzu said in *The Art of War*, "Know yourself and know your enemy, and in 100 battles you shall emerge victorious 100 times."

Practice Taking Risks

The corporate jungle is a competitive place. Spend time developing your risk-taking skills, both personally and professionally, and before long you will be running at the head of the pack.

Remember That It DOES Matter

It is so easy to get comfortable and pretend that the getting paid less (someone will take care of me) and having our actions often go unnoticed (someone will notice soon) isn't such a big deal. Women statistically earn less, live longer and die poorer. Money isn't everything but it does buy you the freedom to live the life you want and the security you crave. And if you're working this hard, don't you think you deserve to enjoy the fruits of your labor.

Rule # 3 Master Jungle Speak

Have you ever felt as though you've said something a million times and still weren't heard? If so, it's time that you learn Jungle Speak, a complex language that incorporates words, gestures, tones and hormonal signals.

Even if you feel as though you're already being heard and respected in the jungle, think about this: by learning to communicate like a monkey, you'll be able to get your message across much more effectively and create instant authority. What's more, it will also become easier and more rewarding for the monkeys to communicate with you, allowing you to move more easily through the corporate jungle.

People only hear 20 percent of what you are saying; the remainder of their perception of you is based on your appearance and your tone. Body language is key but there is a whole other layer to your body language that you do not have direct control over: your hormones.

The truth is that very few people hear what you are saying—rather they *see* what you are saying, so if the various parts of your message are not speaking in unison, you will confuse your audience—or, even worse, anger them.

In this chapter, you'll
• Learn how to speak with impact and be heard
• Overcome the biggest workplace challenge and learn how to deal with someone stealing your work
• Avoid common communication blunders
• Discover what body language mistakes you're making, and how to fix them
• Learn how to respond to negative feedback and antagonism
• Master the hidden language that rules the corporate jungle

Jungle Speak: The Verbal Part

The first thing you need to know about Jungle Speak is that it is a practical spoken language that has evolved to communicate immediate needs, threats and long-term goals. Things like personal status and territory are often communicated via biological signals rather than spoken language.

As you learned in the last chapter, one of the significant differences between women and men is that women are excellent with language and inclined to being–as many men perceive it–overly expressive and thoughtful, bordering on neurotic.

The monkeys in the corporate jungle have limited mental diversity and are primarily occupied with tangible goals and imminent threats. To them, each spoken word is endowed with powerful meaning and urgency, so when you approach the monkeys and start rambling off a long string of words, they soon become exhausted or frustrated and tune you out.

This is often what happens when you approach a monkey and preface what you need or share your thoughts rather than plans.

Remember, it's crucial to keep things simple and avoid unnecessary inflections and hidden meanings that might confuse them or be lost on them. You'll be saving both parties a lot of trouble that way.

Five Reasons the Monkeys Don't Hear You

Ever feel like you talk all day and nothing gets done? Like you've discussed a problem and come up with solutions, but nothing changes? Rest assured: so does everyone else. There are five common communication killers that happen in every single conversation we have, both at home and at work.

While all of us know how to talk, few people truly know how to communicate, leading to a lot of confusion, misunderstanding and friction. But don't be too hard on yourself. We are one of the few species that's mastered verbal communications, and we deal with a lot more than our friends the dolphins.

Here are five of the biggest communication killers and their antidotes:

You're Not Anticipating Needs and Filters

The most common communications fires are caused by people not recognizing, considering or respecting other people's filters. If the person you are talking to is stressed or has poor self-esteem, a perfectly neutral message may be perceived as an aggressive or passive-aggressive threat. If a person is full of themselves or living in a self-serving fantasy world, even a criticism that is phrased too kindly may be received as a compliment.

Memorize this rule: communications are never about you. Communications are always about the other person and getting something from them, so you had better phrase your message in a way that they are happy and willing to receive.

Whenever possible, spend some time ahead of your meeting to get clear on your message and how you are going to phrase it. If you're dealing with someone who is very stressed and you have to add more work to his plate, start by thanking him for his hard work, and then make a suggestion for how it could be improved, rather than immediately informing him what's wrong with it. If your boss is insanely busy but you need an answer, don't give her the full report, but rather offer up a one-paragraph summary with a link to the full report, and a clearly phrased question you need answered, if there is one.

You're Sending Mixed Messages

The side effect of being a species with highly developed verbal communication skills is that we often forget that much of our communication takes place through our bodies. When we are sick, stressed or anxious, we not only change our body language but also our chemical makeup, sending big, flashing warning signals to those around us. This in turn makes us less popular, especially with women whose senses are more honed in to these kinds of signals.

The perception of strength, health and control can provide an added oomph and validity to whatever it is that you're talking about, so before your next meeting, find a private spot and practice the Wonder Woman and Victory poses described at the end of this chapter and try to reduce your stress. It's not only good for your body, but good for your career.

You're Being Too Vague or Too Specific

You may be tempted to show off just how much you know with a long report or presentation, but beware of overloading your audience. Some bosses love it but many monkeys don't have time for it, and if you show them anything longer than a simple summary and some fancy infographics, their eyes will glaze over and your brilliant paper will end up at the bottom of their to do pile, or worse, their doo-doo pile.

Learn the communications styles of your colleagues and superiors, and cater to them. Yes, it's added work, but when your ideas and words resonate, they will have a far greater impact, saving you a ton of effort in the long run. Bullet points are a very effective and efficient way to detail information on emails, and for super-busy superiors, I often make a yes/no checklist that they can plow through without having to waste time in meetings. In most cases, they are pleased that someone has thought to make their lives easier.

You're Too "Busy"

In our ever-competitive world we developed the notion that working 7 a.m. to 10 p.m. should be the status quo and that you can only prove your chops if you're continually outstaying your colleagues at the office. While some bosses appreciate you running yourself ragged for their company, the truth is that being "busy" and working late can easily be interpreted as being inefficient. The result? People avoid you because you're already too stressed and busy to give them any real attention, and your office relationships wilt because people assume that you have no time for them.

The antidote? First, keep your stress in check. Second, when people come to talk to you, put down what you're doing, turn away from the computer or smartphone screen and devote your entire attention to them. If you're really smart, you'll also preface the conversation with "You know, I'm really busy, but I'd love to have this talk with you," which will immediately boost their egos, and with it, their opinion of you!

They're "Hangry"

As much as we can't ignore the other person's psychological filters, biological influences can be just as powerful, if not more so. A recent study by Ohio State University psychology researcher Brad Bushman found that people with low blood sugar tended to have much less self-control, which in turn caused them to lash out at their partners more frequently. The researchers call this being "hangry." It's no secret that sleep deprivation can have the same effects on our self-control.

So if you find yourself butting heads with the monkeys in your afternoon meetings, consider that either party may have burned through their energy for the day. Consider having some bananas or walking to a coffee shop and see if things improve.

Be Straightforward

There's an unbelievable amount of time and energy wasted on miscommunication because people expect monkeys to read between the lines.

A highly evolved species like yourself can read the subtleties in body language, facial expressions and yes, the underlying meaning of what is being said. Some monkeys can do so as well, but often don't see the clues as relevant or important because they expect those around them to say what they are thinking.

This means that when you approach a monkey and tell them that your report will be late because you don't have enough resources, only a small fraction of them will realize that you are indirectly asking for more resources. Instead, they may assume that you are not smart enough to make due with what you've got. A much safer approach to addressing this topic is to tell them that there are not enough resources to finish the project and that more are needed. This subtle difference in phrasing implies a situational problem rather than a personal problem.

If you're shocked or terrified by this idea, take a moment to turn inside and try to figure out why this is so intimidating to you. Are you afraid that you will be perceived as needy or demanding? Inefficient? Are you afraid of rejection? Don't be! Your only job in the jungle is to get the job done, and if there is something you require to accomplish that, the jungle will provide for you. The worst possible thing that could happen is that you may be denied, and even that will be soon forgotten, so just go for it!

On the flip side, the obsession with reading deeper meanings into our work interactions is highly destructive, as it often sends women into a tailspin trying to discover the true meaning of what is being said. The truth is, there aren't that many things that are left unsaid in the workplace, and most of them don't matter as long as you're getting what you need out of the jungle and vice versa. So the next time you suspect that something is "being said" take a deep breath, relax and accept that if it was important enough to share with you, the monkey probably would be more direct.

One of the defining moments in my own career took place when a professional trainer disciplined one of my monkey colleagues during a meeting. For months our leadership team had been trying to work around this colleague, whose dominance in meetings and the office space brought about good results, but often at great cost to office morale. We'd tried everything to bridge the gap between his team and other departments, but he was firmly of the opinion that since his product was exceptional, he shouldn't waste any time trying to cooperate with management or take part in the company culture.

After a training session held by the consultant he leaned back in his chair, crossed his arms and told her he didn't think it was for him. He challenged her on whether or not "this stuff" really worked. She explained to him that it did, and rattled off an impressive list of clients and achievements. "Of course you'd say that" he scoffed, "after all, you're the one who's selling it."

The trainer stood up tall (marking her physical space), put her hands on her hips and let him have it! She reminded him that she wasn't selling anything, that the leaders of the company had brought her in to do a job, and if he didn't like it, he was welcome to leave the company at any time.

In her first big meeting she had said the one thing that everyone had been dying to say but was afraid to, and it worked! For the first time he realized that people didn't like his attitude and really only put up with him because he got things done. He also realized that this reign of terror had gone on too long, and that it was time to play by the company rules, which included not antagonizing others.

While he never turned into a cute and cuddly chimp, I didn't have any other staff members quit the team because they didn't want to work in the same office as him, and that was a huge win. All it took was one moment of complete honesty, coupled with the correct body language and tone.

Make It Snappy

Jungle time is extremely is limited–or at least the monkeys seem to think it is. Everyone is forever in a rush to find bananas or escape danger, so if you want to be heard, you need to make sure that your messages are both clear and concise.

The challenge that many women face is that they are waiting for the jungle to tell them what their roles should be, rather than asserting what their roles are and seizing them. Our biology and upbringing are the culprits here, and our infinite flexibility and adaptability means we are often left second-guessing what we should be doing. Defining who you are can be a challenge, but certainly one worth taking on for the many benefits that knowing the answer will provide.

My favorite resource for getting to know yourself and your talents is the book *Go Put Your Strengths to Work* which teaches that you should actively do those things that make you happy, where you lose all sense of time and leave feeling immensely satisfied.

To get started on the path to greater clarity and communications, you need to develop your office "elevator pitch." To start, create a one-sentence statement for each of the following questions:

Who am I and what do I do?
What is it that I do *for* this company?
Where do I see myself in five years?

If I could retire today with everything I need, what would my life be like?

Once you have the answers to these questions, you'll be able to impress anyone who wants to know who you are with your vision and drive, including yourself.

Flip Your Arguments

Part of having great clarity in your speech is doing the opposite of what you're likely doing now: instead of prefacing your statements, you need to make them directly, and follow up with any other information only if necessary. Not only does this send a more powerful message and show self-awareness, it also frees the monkeys from deciphering your preamble, which they often feel is a waste of their precious time. All monkeys like being told the answers and the bottom line up front.

To do this, think about what you are going to say beforehand, isolate your key points and approach the monkey with a clear and simple phrase, such as: "I need x and y so that I can z." Stay clear from the need to justify your requests. If your intentions are clear and pertinent, the monkey has no reason to deny you.

Speak with Importance and Conviction

The most common mistake made by non-native speakers of Jungle Speak is prefacing what you are about to say with belittling agents, such as:

- I think
- I feel

65

- I would like to
- Um
- I'm sorry, but
- Can I
- I may be wrong here
- I was thinking
- So…
- I just…
- Or "just" in any context, for that matter.
- other sounds, like laughing before or after you make a statement

When you preface your thoughts with these words, you are indicating that what you are saying is not important or concrete. When communicating with monkeys, you must always stick to the facts, in order of importance, and remove all the surrounding fluff words. Doing so makes you sound credible, self-assured and confident (even when you personally think you sound a bit rude).

To the monkey's ears, all of these conversational fillers are useless garble and make it very clear that you are uncertain of your convictions and require leadership and assistance in your decision-making process. If that's the case, your supervising monkey might promote a younger, bolder monkey ahead of you based on the sole fact that he or she is brazen, or in their eyes, a natural leader.

So what should you do when you're feeling less than self-assured in your decision and actually *do* need advice? Follow Vogue editor-in-chief Anna Wintour's advice: just make a decision and act as though it is the right thing to do.

In an office situation, that means presenting your well thought-out arguments to the monkey for his opinion. He'll be grateful that you didn't treat him like a personal bouncing board for your ideas and waste his time, and will also get an ego boost from sharing his thoughts and will admire you for taking his feedback so well (reaffirming his ego). The result: a plan that everyone loves.

Responding to Criticism and Failure

Have you ever been told to "man up" and face criticism or failure? Don't take this personally because it has nothing to do with the possession or lack of certain genitalia, but rather an ingrained communication style. To be more precise, the phrase refers to the habit of many women to try to hide and fix a problem or to ameliorate their bosses.

When someone first gives you feedback, your learned response will likely be to apologize and explain what happened, but that can be crippling to your career. When the monkey states a fact ("you messed up"), he is expressing a truth: his truth. When you counter his truth by trying to explain what happened, he sees it as you denying what he believes to be true and undermining him.

The best way to respond to criticism or negative feedback is to accept it graciously, and to offer proof that you are capable of learning and doing a good job by asking for feedback and assuring that the situation will be fixed.

Never offer up an excuse or the reasons for the failure unless expressly asked for those reasons. If you're too quick to do so, you will appear defensive, and depending on the situation, the monkey may only be interested in venting or expressing frustration. If he does ask for reasons, present them with the facts only, and try not to be too hard on yourself or apologize for what happened. You're already in trouble and don't need to make yourself look worse.

Above all, avoid becoming emotional. We all have pressures, but monkeys respond to stress differently than we do, and can get really freaked out by emotional behavior such as crying. If it happens, be sure to let the monkeys know that you won't be losing your composure again. You don't want them to avoid you in the future because you've made them uncomfortable.

So what if a monkey really is wrong in his criticism of you? Depending on the type of monkey you're dealing with, it may be wise to say, "I understand what you're saying. Let me take a look into it and get back to you." This will give you time to formulate a damage-control strategy, but more importantly, you won't be directly antagonizing the monkey's ego. You can come back later and explain the situation, with the added bonus that you will be much calmer and your stress signals won't be making the situation worse.

Above all, remember that the jungle knows no failure. If a mistake doesn't kill you, the next day will offer another chance to prove yourself once again.

Don't Take It Personally

Jungle Speak is direct, practical and unemotional. By now you've mastered talking Jungle Speak but do you know how to respond to it? One of the most common complaints about women in the workplace is that they take things too personally. If you are perceived as being overly sensitive or reactive, the monkeys will learn to keep a distance from you to avoid unnecessary complications and emotional outbursts, both of which give them the chills.

Monkeys live in the moment and don't have a mental filter, so whatever need or feeling they have is often immediately communicated to you without censorship. On the one hand, this makes them a delight to work with, as you can simply respond to their needs without having to spend too much time figuring out what it is they really want.

On the other hand, it means that you may be subject to an outburst or attack. When this happens, keep in mind that this reaction is based on a perceived threat, and that by lashing out, the monkey is creating a safe space and dominance to assure his own status until he can resolve the situation. In short: it's not about you, so don't take it personally.

The question then becomes that if it's not personal, you shouldn't react, right? WRONG! If you don't react to the monkey's outburst, or if you react in a way that the monkey can't understand, he will become confused and develop mistrust in you, because he doesn't understand your actions.

Responding to an outburst or personal attack

with kindness (tend and befriend) raises great suspicion. This is why being nice to your bullies never works.

Remember when we talked about how women deal with stress? Our natural inclination is to harmonize, whereas the monkey deals only in two functions: fight or flight. It is perfectly acceptable for you to retreat, but if you stick around to tend to him, you will become very suspect.

If the monkey is out of line or not your superior, the best way to deal with an outburst may be to stand your ground and fight back. This does not mean taking a low punch, but rather asserting your position and making sure the monkey knows this is your turf. This can be as simple as reminding them that the boss put you there for a reason, or that the thing making them upset really isn't your personal pet project, but something that is best for the company.

I've seen too many perfectly innocuous workplace interactions blow up into a thousand pieces because an individual took something personally. In some cases, an employee suspected their boss didn't respect their work, when in fact there were too many other fires to put out for the boss to give them the feedback they deserved. In other situations, people make the mistake of assuming that harsh words or bad vibes are directed towards them, when in fact, they had nothing to do with the office at all. When you react personally to other people's behavior, you not only deprive them of the benefit of the doubt and the right to have their own feelings, but you also hand them the right to control your emotions on a silver platter.

Even worse, your reaction to their behavior might also trigger a reaction from them or other colleagues, and before you know it, everyone is worked up into a frenzy. If you're lucky, the misunderstanding can be resolved, but if not, you might end up getting pegged as the person who cried wolf and whose howls drove everyone nuts.

This happened with the CEO of a publishing company, who couldn't figure out why his team of senior editors resented him so much. As a typical monkey, he saw no problem storming into their section of the workplace jungle, dumping all of his brilliant ideas on them and then retreating into his own cave to come up with other ways to revolutionize his business. Not once did he think to slow down and ask himself what his sudden outbursts might do to the team. What's more, he rarely followed up on any of his inspirations, so the editors had no idea as to what they should take seriously and what they could ignore.

One editor in particular was very defensive of her work and always took his "suggestions" as a direct criticism of what she was doing. She never told him, of course, and tried her very best to implement contradictory suggestions while slowly letting her resentment of him fester. As you can guess, that wasn't the most productive solution. One day three years into her career she stormed into his office and told him that she was sick of having her work criticized, and that if he thought he could do a better job, he was welcome to take over or hire someone new. Frankly, she'd had enough of late nights and tight budgets anyways!

The CEO was in shock. It has never occurred to him that his positive contributions would be interpreted as criticisms, and what's more, his employee had never brought up workloads or budgets before. The relationship became extremely strained as he no longer knew how to approach her, and eventually another mediator and I had to be called in to repair the relationship.

One crucial difference in men's and women's communications style that often causes these person reactions is the man's constant interruptions. Women—who always seek to understand and empathize—are wonderful listeners, but also skilled complainers. Men on the other hand, are much more eager to resolve the matter quickly, and will often offer suggestions, even when it's not their turn to speak or when they weren't asked. It's easy to see how this could easily send sparks flying, especially in an environment where you're relying on the other person's feedback for your approval and self-esteem.

So remember, the next time something rubs you the wrong way, don't take it personally. If it's something that needs to be addressed, do so honestly, openly and without blame. Any monkey—or human, for that matter—who is antagonized reprimanded in response to what he intended as being helpful (and he may well think teasing, bullying or being a jerk is being helpful) will become very distrustful when he's been insulted for a sincere action. Oftentimes, addressing the offense in an unemotional way is the best way to deal with it and put an end to unwanted behavior.

Don't Make It Personal

We've established that monkeys have a hard time understanding and anticipating your personal feelings, and that's why you shouldn't take things personally. On the flip side, you also shouldn't try to *make* things personal. When you do, you'll be trying to punish someone in a way he won't understand, and even worse, you'll be wasting your energy in passive-aggressive pursuits that don't bear any fruit. Have you ever heard the saying that "resentment is like drinking poison and hoping that it will kill the other person?" It's not worth the trouble.

Be particularly wary of this behavior when you've been let down by a monkey who didn't do what they promised. When this happens, be straightforward and express your disappointment that the task didn't get done, but also your confidence that you know he will do better next time. This will send a direct message, and get the monkey excited to prove himself to you.

Keep Your Feelings on a Tree

Science has proven that talking about experiences changes the way that they are processed in the brain. As women are more susceptible to emotion, reflection and internalization, we are particularly inclined to share our thoughts and feelings with others in order to process them.

But sharing your feelings in the corporate jungle is quite dangerous, as monkeys might interpret your feelings as facts, and before you know it, those feelings become your identity. So unless you know for sure that you have a trusted confidant, keep your feelings etched on a personal tree, or as we call it, a journal.

When you express yourself, remember to choose your words wisely. Your words become your reality, and their negative energy can easily take over your life, or people's opinion of you.

The reality is that even a terrible boss or colleague can teach you resilience and make you a stronger, smarter and more agile person. No one said that life in the jungle would be easy, but it does become more tolerable when we take the challenges we experience and turn them into lessons. Whenever possible, try to reframe any negative experiences with a positive attitude so that you don't build up negative subconscious patterns.

Keep It Low and Slow

Much like body language says more about you than your actual words, the speed and tone with which you speak also send powerful messages about your content.

In recent years, companies such as Jobaline have developed algorithms that analyze your voice and determine whether or not it is appealing and compelling. Al Pacino, it turns out, has an undeniably appealing voice that resonates with all human beings.

Biologically speaking, a low voice is directly related to a higher testosterone level, which in turn is related to higher social standing, dominance and more power. One of the telltale signs that a woman feels less than qualified to lead the pack or sell her own ideas is a spike in the pitch of her voice. If you want to be taken seriously, cultivate the habit of speaking in a low tone whenever you're in an important meeting.

While you're at it, you'll also want to regulate how quickly you speak: speaking slowly shows your audience that you're in control, confident and thoughtful, whereas speaking quickly sends the message that you're frightened, panicked and excitable. Every time you're getting ready to speak to others, make sure you take a deep breath and speak more slowly than you think you should.

Work the Silence

Your biological inclination is to make everyone feel completely at ease. The problem is, this sets you up to be a friend or a mother, but certainly not a manager. One of the easiest ways to give the impression that you are a powerful force is to work the silence. Instead of filling small gaps in conversation with reassuring nods and words, sit still, keep your eyes on the subject, listen carefully, and, once he is done speaking, allow at least 3 seconds before you respond. Doing so not only raises the level of respect he will feel for you, but also sends a strong message that you are thoughtful, intelligent and in charge of the situation.

One of the women I worked with through a mentorship program is perhaps the nicest woman I have ever met, though you wouldn't know this when you first meet her. A young entrepreneur, she sold her first company for a few million dollars before the age of 25 (and while I've never asked, I've always attributed her poker face to her success at a young age).

When I first met her, I could have sworn she didn't like me. We were at a networking event and everyone there was drinking and smiling but her. We met, were introduced and I left the conversation feeling as though I may have rubbed her the wrong way.

One of my friends knew her personally, and in a moment of insecurity, I called my friend and asked why this woman would have treated me that way and why she didn't like me. After all, we didn't even know each other! My friend burst out laughing and said that she got this question all the time. "That's just how she is! Give her some time and you'll see how amazing she is!"

My friend did not steer me wrong. As I got to know this woman better, I learned that she wasn't in the habit of smiling for no reason, but that when she did, it was always sincere and radiant.

When I was getting ready to make an international move, I called her and asked if she could give me a crash course in international investments. I'd heard rumors that she was incredibly savvy in this area. She invited me to her house for lunch, and proceeded to teach me everything she knew. I still have pages and pages of notes from that meeting, but what I remember most is my head spinning on the way home. Sitting in the taxicab, it occurred to me that by not befriending everyone who crossed her path, she was able to pour her energies into relationships that really mattered and truly make an impact on other people's lives, and she was *always* taken seriously.

Use Words to Protect Your Work

One of the most common complaints coming from the corporate jungle is that people are not being given due credit for their work.

If you are outspoken, verbal and communicative, then all of the relevant people in your company should know who you are and what you do, making it very difficult for others to steal your work in the first place.

That being said, there will be times when someone steals your work or "forgets" to give you credit in a meeting. When this happens, your gut instinct may be to complain about how someone stole your work, but the truth is that the corporate jungle doesn't care who did the work, as long as it got done. The only way to salvage the situation is to add value. To do so, lean in and point out something that you found working on the project that the thief may have omitted. This requires a lot of finesse, but also gives you a chance to show off your brilliance. Just don't be condescending, or else the thief may lash out.

Jungle Speak: the Biological Aspect

Human language is a relatively new invention, and before we were able to communicate complex concepts with words, our bodies took care of the job with body language and biological signals.

The beauty of our biological signals–hormones and pheromones–is that they were designed to be subtle yet powerful enough to communicate the most vital information to the people around us. All of these signals evolved to protect the species from extinction, so they communicate the most pressing human concerns: reproduction and survival.

You may wonder what the two have to do with your life in the corporate jungle. While they aren't related to your weekly report, hormones and pheromones will directly influence how others perceive you *and* the report, and may determine whether or not anyone takes you seriously when you present it.

Controlling Your Pheromone Flares

While hormones can have a positive influence on your office life, you need to be aware of the dark side to your body's secret communication. If you're stressed, unhappy or sick, your body will send out pheromonal flares alerting those around you to the impeding danger of attack and disease. This biological warning system was designed to protect you and your clan, but if you suffer from chronic stress, the people you most want to connect with may associate you with being a threat and keep their distance from you.

As you know, stress is your body's natural

reaction to danger. It draws blood and tension to your muscles, sharpens your perception and raises adrenaline and cortisol levels so that you can deal with the impeding danger, be it a deadline, an office conflict or a tiger. Stress is extremely useful in small doses as your pheromones will alert the rest of your pack that it's time to get off their rumps and get stuff done.

But when you're facing chronic stress, your body loses the ability to find relief, which is a natural part of the stress cycle during which adrenaline and cortisol are broken down. This causes cortisol build-up and adrenal fatigue, which destroy your energy, your immune system and your overall health, as well as impairing your cognitive functions. You become hyper-vigilant (since adrenaline only allows you to focus on the problem at hand), agitated and eventually you burn out.

Cortisol is also extremely disruptive to your sleep patterns and a build-up can cause insomnia, which in turn will amplify all of your problems. As you fall apart mentally and physically, the people around you will come to associate you with stress and will start breaking off ties with you to protect themselves from the perceived threat. But it is not only your colleagues that might pick up on your moods via your scent. Recent research has shown that people unconsciously smell their palms after shaking someone's hands for the first time as their inner ape tries to assess vital information about the new person in their network.

Sometimes even when we're trying our best to hide it, our stresses from home can carry into the workplace. One senior sales and marketing manager I interviewed noticed this happening inside her team. Despite the fact that everyone was doing well and that people were lining up to hand them money, one of her top sales executive's numbers were dropping, and no one could explain why. Her calls hadn't changed, and certainly there had been no client complaints.

When she dug deeper and contacted some of the clients who were buying less, she noticed that none of them had a reason for doing so–they just didn't feel as secure in the brand as they had previously. It wasn't until she sat down with her sales executive that she noticed a very subtle yet distinct change in that executive's vibe. The words that were coming out of her mouth hadn't changed, but whereas before she'd always radiated confidence and enthusiasm, there was now an air of defeat and an anxiety that subtly lurked in her tone.

When the manager asked the sales executive how she was doing outside of work, she casually mentioned that she'd been through a stressful breakup, but that it wasn't a big deal. If anything, it had given her more time to focus on her clients.

While the sales executive wasn't aware of it, the stress from the breakup had influenced her work on a subconscious level. While she wasn't particularly distraught about the end of her relationship *per se*, the stress of processing the breakup had imprinted itself on her biology and was sending a subtle distress signal to her regular clients, who in turn lowered their commitments because of the insecurity that she was projecting.

When you're suffering from any kind of stress, you are likely to send out those same signals, so be

honest with yourself and practice some of the de-
stressing and confidence boosting exercises from this
book to prevent the damage from spreading to your
network.

One way to deal with stress and bond is to give
an imaginary hug. Hugs release a powerful hormone
called oxytocin, which increases your empathy, trust
and generosity. There are very few situations in which
it is appropriate to hug your colleagues or your bosses,
but studies have shown that even delivering an
imaginary hug will raise your level of oxytocin, which
can lower your stress level and make you feel more
comfortable with your audience. Some research also
suggests that it helps people bond, meaning you'll
endear yourself to them on a biological level.

Leverage Your Fertility

Most of us are unaware of the signals our bodies are
sending without our knowledge, and for women one of
the biggest signals by far is "Hello world! I'm fertile!"

Scientific studies have shown that men find fertile
women more attractive, and that women also feel more
confident and attractive when they are ovulating
(which usually occurs between 12 and 14 days before
your period starts).

During ovulation, your ovaries dump a massive
amount of estrogen into your bloodstream. Estrogen is
a hormone that is directly linked to serotonin
production and mood. You feel on top of the world,
are outgoing, and, believe it or not, you are smarter!
Plus women experience a slight spike in testosterone

around the time of ovulation, which makes you bolder and more willing to take risks. Do you see why this is the perfect time to talk to your boss about that raise?

So why not leverage this double-sided boost in your attractiveness and confidence to accelerate your professional career, and schedule key appointments around this time of the month?

Not only will you feel better, more outgoing and magnetic during this time, but your male colleagues will also feel much more inclined to make you happy. Plus, if you're afflicted with periodic mood swings, it certainly won't hurt for you to avoid certain other times of the month.

Working around ovulation and your estrogen peaks certainly beats trying to communicate with anyone when progesterone is wreaking havoc with your body right before your period. When this happens, you're biologically programmed to turn inward to seek safety and stability, and are unlikely to rock the boat.

But don't curse your hormones just yet, because this tendency to retreat may protect your career. Other known effects of progesterone include forgetfulness and a lowered ability to express yourself, so it's not the best time to put yourself out there anyway.

If you don't know your cycle yet, learn it now, and start leveraging the power of your fertile days. Don't forget to forgive yourself when you're having an off day. You can finally, and with scientific proof, blame it on your hormones. Just don't do so in public, because the monkeys will think you're crazy.

Here's another interesting fact related to fertility: according to one study, women were more likely to underperform on Mondays because they were preoccupied with the fact that they didn't use birth control properly over the weekend. Make of that what you will, but don't you think it's convenient that taking charge of your fertility and reproductive health can now be counted as a career booster?

How to Deal with Bullies

Have you ever noticed how some people give you a "stay away" vibe from the moment you walk into their offices? Chances are, you're picking up both on their physical and biological cues, all of which are intended to communicate the relationship between the two of you and determine who's really in charge. If you happen to be threatening to a person—and there are a number of reasons this could happen—you might find yourself at the brunt of his or her terror with no apparent reason or explanation. This is commonly known as having a bully.

So how you do deal with people who seem to have it out for you for no apparent reason? First of all, you cannot try to befriend them or win them over. Bullying is a form of antagonism, and no jungle creature on the planet responds to an enemy attack by trying to make friends with the aggressors. It's unnatural, and often the antagonizing parties will become more mistrustful of you as they perceive you as trying to con them into winning their trust.

The real way to deal with bullies is to confront them, whether it is submissively or aggressively. By choosing to act submissively, you acknowledge that they are in charge, and can continue to work with them in a way that doesn't threaten them. While this isn't ideal, there are some bullies who control your career, so it's necessary to keep their egos intact.

Ideally, however, you confront the bullies and stake your turf. This involves pointing out the unprofessional behavior (though try to avoid calling it unprofessional unless it's a severe case) and the fact that it interferes with your work. Remember, while the corporate jungle is a loaded minefield of relationships, the bottom line is always the work. Keep your emotions out of this conversation, no matter how hurt you may be. And trust me: if you always focus on the work and the goals, you will be heard.

Jungle Speak: the Physical Aspect

The physical aspect of Jungle Speak is what people commonly refer to as "non-verbal" communication or body language: the signs your body sends through its posture and movements. This is more important than the biological aspect of your communications, and the two of them actually have a mutually dependent relationship, meaning that if you work on one, the other will automatically improve.

For instance, one German study found that if you raise your line of sight above the horizon or force your face into a smile, your body responds by releasing hormones that increase happiness. The opposite is true when people are forced into a slumped or hunched position with their eyes on the ground: the body, responding to the signal that the person is depressed and lacks energy, makes sure that the hormones are thinking the same thing, and testosterone and serotonin start to drop in response.

But the impacts of your physical body language are not just internal; they also send powerful signals to those around you about who you are, how powerful you are and what their relationship to you should be. These signals are emitted by every part of your body, so let's start from the top-down and correct some of the bad habits you may currently practice.

Common Body Language Misinterpretations

Humans are one of the few creatures in the world with enough psychological and linguistic complexity to lie, which is why psychologists, the police and even recruiters are all trained in watching your body language to find out what you're *really* thinking.

But when people talk about body language, they often have an overly simple understanding of the science, and what's more, aren't aware of common habits (including poor posture) that can easily present a false reading.

Below are some common body language misinterpretations, as well as some guidelines for truly conveying your message.

	Posture	**Message**
Legs	Sitting with legs crossed	Defensive, hiding
	Sitting with legs apart	Open, confident, relaxed
	Kicking legs	Bored, annoyed
	Locked ankles	Scared, resentful

	Posture	**Message**
Arms	Arms crossed on chest	Rejection
	Hands on hips, arms spread out	Powerful, mildly aggressive and/or defensive

	Posture	Message
Head	Tilted head	Contemplation
	Tilted head with moving of hair	Submission
	Playing with hair	Submission, insecurity

	Posture	Message
Hands	Rubbing hands	Thinking, indecision
	Steepled hands	Power, contemplation
	Playing with hands	Bored, disengaged
	Using hands to cover your mouth or touch your nose	Hiding something, insecure
	Touching your face or ears	Contemplation
	Hands in pocket	Anxiety, insecurity
	Biting nails	Anxiety, insecurity
	Hands behind back	Insecurity, hiding
	Hands locked in front	Insecurity
	Showing the palms of your hands	Openness, security, collaboration

One way to keep an eye on your body language is to record yourself sitting at your desk giving an imaginary speech or being interviewed. Play back your video and pay attention to your body, really noticing how you feel when you make certain gestures. Many people don't realize that they have small, nervous tics that will give them away in this kind of situation.

Put your Best Face Forward

Did you know that Princess Diana used to spend hours practicing her expressions in a mirror? While the Princess of Wales was one of the most enchanting women known to the public eye, she wasn't born that way. Her biographer revealed that she spent endless hours studying photos and practicing facial expressions to perfect her image and project a refined, elegant and confident façade.

Women are extremely adept at reading other people's faces, and even though the importance of this skill has become less relevant with the advent of the spoken word, our expressions are still powerful presentations of ourselves.

Stop Smiling

Forget everything your mother and Dale Carnegie taught you about approaching people with a smile. The truth is that it sends the wrong message. When you're constantly smiling at everyone, it tells them that you are fully content with the way things are, and that they need not make an effort to impress you.

Practice projecting a kind expression, but save your smile for later in the conversation. Not only does this create authority, but it also creates a more favorable impression, as the person you're speaking with will believe your smile was reserved for her alone.

Watch Your Eyes

Our eyes are powerful messengers, and lack of eye contact is a sign of submission. If you have trouble holding a steady gaze, you might be perceived as a pushover, or even worse, elusive and dishonest. Most people actually reported having a more positive opinion of the person they were speaking with when their partner focused intently on them.

When you're meeting with someone, make sure that you hold eye contact at least 80 percent of the time, and if you need practice, then get it. An easy way to do this is to pull up an image of someone on your computer screen and have a staring contest with that person.

All that being said, you do want to make sure not to hold eye contact when you're in trouble with a superior, as this will come off as aggressive and might heighten the tension.

Stop Tilting Your Head

Have you ever noticed how your dog tilts its head when you are talking? Your dog is showing you submission by exposing his neck, and humans, especially women, tend to do the same thing, both by tilting their heads and moving their hair away from their necks. This action immediately undermines the woman's authority and can inflate the ego of the other party. When you want to be taken seriously, you need to keep your head on straight and avoid flipping your hair from your neck, another sign of submission.

You should also check to make sure you're not nodding too much, another common sign of submission and indecisiveness. A well-timed nod will have a much more powerful effect in establishing group cohesion without compromising your role.

Walk the Right Way
When you enter a new space for the first time, the one element that is immediately visible to others is the way you walk. A study conducted in the 1980's by two researchers from New York City asked criminals to watch a series of videos and judge whether or not they would target the people shown.

As it turns out, those with too small or too large a gait and those who didn't use their whole bodies when they walked (limiting their arm and torso movements) were perceived as more vulnerable. The same is true in the workplace, where that kind of body language immediately classifies you as submissive and frightened.

The Best Posture for Office Meetings

Have you ever noticed what happens to kids, dogs and coworkers when they are scolded? They shrink down into themselves and dip backwards—a clear sign of submission and shame. What about a woman on a first date, or a puppy who's happy to see you? They perk up, tilt their heads and show off their necks—clear signs of submission.

Now think your own posture. Do you slouch, take up a small space or lean sideways in your chair? If you do, you're sending everyone around you the message that you're lacking in energy, confidence and authority, all of which are critical to workplace success. The next time before you enter the room, remember to stick out your chest and roll your shoulders back, which is jungle speak for being in charge.

Raise Your Chin

A raised chin has always been associated with pride and confidence, but do you know why? When you raise your chin, you automatically push down your shoulders (a sign of certainty and confidence) and open up your sternum, broadening your chest. This in and of itself portrays confidence, but it also deepens your breathing, which in turn relaxes you, and nothing creates confidence like being relaxed in a situation.

And remember, raising your chin, your gaze and your field of vision triggers serotonin production, another precursor to confidence and happiness. Be sure to make this one of your go-to habits.

Tuck Your Shoulders Back

Your shoulders can also tell your audience a lot about what you are feeling, but unfortunately our shoulders also tend to be the biggest liars. Lack of exercise and endless hours spent hunched in front of the computer have warped our spines and weakened our stomach muscles so that sitting or standing up tall takes real effort. Chances are that your body is so accustomed to slouching that you often fall back into bad habits and communicate, "I'm tired, I'm weak and I lack authority."

If you want to change your body language to project confidence, you'll either have to make a concerted effort to focus on your body language during meetings (when you should really be focusing on what's happening *at* the meeting), or you'll have to train your body to project confidence on a regular basis.

Luckily, this is easier said than done: simply raise your computer monitor to encourage you to look straight ahead rather than downward, and, if possible, support your lower back so that your spine and chest arch slightly forward and push your shoulders down and back.

Leaning In vs. Leaning Back

Sheryl Sandberg made waves with her book *Lean In*, and rightfully so. It was a brilliant call to action empowering women to say "yes" to both their careers and their families without guilt or hesitation. But her book might better be called *Charge!* as leaning in isn't always the best position for doing business in the jungle.

When you physically lean in to a conversation, it shows great interest and also sends a message of affirmation to your audience. While there is a time and place for that, always leaning in to your conversations undermines your authority by telling others that you're too agreeable.

Instead, you might want to try leaning back, a posture that conveys both authority and hesitation. When you lean back at a meeting, you're not only sending the message that you are a person worthy of being won over, you'll also make a much greater impact when you finally do lean in and show your approval.

How to Handle Your Hands

Women are often taught that their hands make a powerful first impression, and that this is why they should get manicures. Sure, having chewed up fingernails is a professional no-no, but chances are good that if your gestures are powerful enough, no one will notice what color nail polish you're sporting.

Unfortunately, many of us misuse our hands in the office, doing things like covering our mouths (which sends the message that you're hiding something or are afraid to speak), flipping our hair, hiding our hands under the table or keeping them in our pockets. All of these send messages of uncertainty and lack of authority.

If you're guilty of these manual crimes, remember these simple rules to improve your image:

• Always keep your hands on the table or at chest level. One good way to start is to keep one hand on the table at all times, which shows that you're engaged and claiming your space.
• If you need to do something with your hands, steeple them and keep them under your chin. This sends a signal of contemplation and authority.
• Use them when you talk. Taking up space, even when it's in mid-air, shows confidence and authority.

The Perfect Handshake
Another gesture that will often belie your true intentions is your handshake. A limp handshake

immediately sends the signal that you're weak, but an excessively strong one might be perceived as a sign of aggression. The rules for the perfect handshake are simple: firm, direct and long. Be sure to hang in there long enough to convey that you're confident, devoted to the mission and not afraid of touching greatness. And remember, touch releases oxytocin and bonding hormones, so a firm, long handshake will also ingratiate you to the other party on a subconscious level.

When it comes to handshakes, beware of the common dominance trick: many super-alpha monkeys will extend their hands with their palms facing down, as a true sign of aggression and dominance. If your fellow hand-shaker is really set on doing this, there is nothing you can do about it, but if you're determined to show him you're a force to be reckoned with, simply give that hand a quick tilt as you shake it, look him in the eye and give him a slight smile. If you're subtle yet persistent enough, the monkey will be intrigued by the challenge of working with you.

Choose Your Seat Wisely

Did you know that where you sit is nearly as important as how you sit? While experts recommend sitting next to the leader of the group, the real power position is actually in his line of sight. Richard Wiseman, professor for Public Understanding of Psychology, writes about the phenomenon in which we unconsciously assume those sitting in the middle are more important than those on the periphery.

There are only two circumstances in which you

should sit close to the leader of a group, rather than opposite that person. The first is when there is an internal conflict and you want to show alignment with the leadership, and the second is when you're feeling less than brilliant and don't want to be noticed.

You'll also want to avoid facing a window when the sun is shining. If you're staring into it, your eyes will be zapped by bright sunlight and you'll quickly feel fatigued, not to mention squinting might make you seem skeptical.

Never Turn Your Back

No animal in the wild ever turns his back on the group, and neither should you, because it sends a signal to your audience that you are vulnerable and open for attack. If you walk into a room and turn your back, it also breaks the energy and diminishes your presence, and can send the subconscious signal that you are not engaged with your audience.

If you're giving a presentation, make sure that your body always remains at least perpendicular to the screen. If you need to look at the screen, move behind your audience (a powerful move in and of itself, as you are asserting yourself over them) and invest in a remote clicker or ask someone to manage the slides for you.

How to Enter a Room

People begin judging you the moment you walk into a room, and unfortunately, women already place themselves at a disadvantage by wearing skirts and heels and carrying purses, all of which slow us down, occupy our hands and disempower us.

Luckily, entering a room in a way that conveys

poise, confidence and power is easier than you'd think–
you just have to relearn everything you know about
opening a door. So what's the best way to enter a
room? Take your purse in your left hand, and open
and push the door with your right hand. This will
automatically keep your right hand open for a
powerful handshake.

Master the Power Poses

Now you understand how mastering your posture is
one of the most powerful things you can do for your
career, and it's time that you learn how to amplify its
power. Harvard Business School Professor Amy Cuddy
discusses the power that our posture has to change our
life by altering our brain chemistry, especially if
practiced with consistency and frequency. That way,
you're training your brain to automatically fire those
neurons that remind you of your confidence, rather
than having to persuade it to act repeatedly.

In her 2012 TED Talk, Cuddy outlines two
specific poses that anyone looking to work in the jungle
should master: The Victory Pose and the Wonder
Woman Pose. Both of these poses, when held for two
minutes at a time, have shown powerful effects on a
person's brain, which in turn changes expression and
performance.

The Victory Pose
Stand with your feet firmly on the ground, lift your
chin and raise your arms into the air, as though you've
just scored a soccer goal. Interestingly, Cuddy's studies
found that even those who were born without sight

assumed this position when they felt victorious, showing just how innate this power pose is to us.

The Wonder Woman Pose

Stand with your feet hips' width apart and firmly planted on the ground. Puff out your chest, and place your hands firmly on your hips. Taking up space is a natural power pose that has a strong effect on your biology, lowering your cortisol and raising your testosterone, thus powerfully preparing you to meet any situation.

Recap: Master Jungle Speak

Go Loud and Low, Simple and Slow

Fast, high-pitched speech is primally associated with danger and excitement, but if you fail to deliver a threat or a party, your fellow jungle mates will soon stop taking you seriously. The best approach is to always go low, slow, loud and simple—the speech pattern of powerful authority figures, and to save the high-speed chatter for when you really need it.

Don't Belittle Yourself

Monkeys are literal creatures and don't always understand the subtleties of human language. When you say you're not good enough, too fat, or could have done better, they will take your word for it. So just tell them what they need to hear, and don't be shy about telling them how awesome you really are. Generally speaking, they won't notice on their own.

Watch Your Body Language

The best investment you can make in your career is to train your body language to present an image of confidence, strength and competence at all times. Don't think of this as being fake, but retraining a lifetime of wimpy habits that make you look bad.

Use Your Body to Get Ahead

At the end of the day, we're all just animals. Get to know your body and eliminate the negative signals you're sending out because of stress and illness. Use your fertility cycle and your natural gifts to get that extra edge you deserve.

Develop Powerful Habits

None of the things you've learned in this chapter are hard–the real challenge is overcoming your ingrained long-term habits to make these actions part of who you are. Even mastering a small portion of these habits can make a big change in your life. If you don't know where to start, make posture and language your top priority, and start seeing immediate effects.

Rule # 4 Work with Your Body

We've already talked about the signals your body sends to others, but it's equally important to understand the signals your body is sending to you. Our bodies are the only true allies we have in the jungle, and nonetheless we often completely ignore them. When we learn to pay attention to the signals our bodies are sending, we'll not only be a lot happier and healthier and overcome some of the physical hurdles that are so common in the workplace–stress, fatigue, anxiety and depression–but we can also supercharge our performance by unleashing that unstoppable animal energy.

So ask yourself: what do you feel like? Do you have aches and pains? Are you fatigued? Or are you alive and buzzing with energy, fully engaged in your job and your life? Are you radiating passion and vivacity?

If you're in the former camp, don't blame yourself. The reason so many women suffer from these problems much more than men is that they adapt themselves to their environment and sacrifice their own needs in order to take care of the group. When we suppress our needs and choose not to express ourselves, we put clamps on our energy, and these blocks of energy eventually become the aches and pains that afflict so many of us. Combine that with our already heightened sensitivities, and it becomes clear why so many women report being unhappy at work.

Fortunately, changing negative and stressful energy is simple when you take a few decided actions.

As you progress, your body will also unlearn and release old stresses that have been making you ill. Before you know it, your mind and body will both be on the same level, and you'll be ready to take the jungle on headfirst.

In this chapter, you'll
• Understand your body's hidden hormonal language and make sure you're sending the right messages
• Learn to control stress and redirect it into energy
• Speak the truth to improve your happiness and power in the office
• Exercise to increase your presence and charisma
• Sleep your way to the top
• Eat your way to a smarter, healthier you
• Develop an infallible gut

Why We Love Stress

A little bit of stress can give you a much-needed boost. As your deadline looms, your senses heighten, you feel energized and tingly all over and you are confident that you can take on the world. That is what stress is designed to do, and why we get hooked on it.

But stress has a dark side as well. Our modern workplace, with its sense-amplifying lights and hyper-efficient machines, has turned us into adrenaline junkies, who swap sleep for sitcoms to calm us down at night and coffee to perk us up in the morning. We enjoy the rush, and even more so, we enjoy being martyrs who prove our exceptional worth by working long and hard hours. Sadly, all this stress takes a real toll on our bodies, which can make us less productive and influential in work over the long run.

The Negative Impacts of Stress

Stress Makes You Narrow-Minded

Both stress and depression share one particular characteristic: the excessive focus and fixation on one particular topic. This function was designed to allow our ancestors to devote all of their attention to the problem at hand and resolve it as soon as possible. That fixation, along with the related symptoms, would end when they figured out what to do. Unfortunately, our modern stresses can seem everlasting, causing us to lose sight of the big picture and creating extreme mental fatigue.

Stress Makes You Ugly

Both men and women are biologically more attracted to calm partners who promise to produce healthy offspring. One of the ways stress makes women less attractive is by decreasing their fertility, which, as you know, has a powerful influence on your charisma.

Elevated stress levels also direct blood flow to your vital organs, meaning your hair, skin and fingernails aren't getting supplied with vital nutrients and will slowly grow dry and brittle.

When this happens, your skin produces excess oil, leading to breakouts, and as the stress ruins the protein caps on your chromosomes, your skin begins to age prematurely and dulls from the exposure to all that excess cortisol.

Stress Makes You Unpopular

Excessive stress can also be categorized as a type of fear, which triggers your body to release hormones to alert those around you of the impending danger. When this goes on for a while, people will notice that they feel worse when they are around you, and will begin instinctually avoiding you.

Stress Makes You Fat

And we're not talking the good kind of fat, which radiates abundance and joy. No, we're talking the unhealthy fat that amasses around your midsection as your body prepares for the worst. This kind of fat is coupled with a loss of muscle mass and bone density, caused by elevated levels of cortisol, and is extremely destructive in the long run.

Stress Makes You Stupid

When you're stressed, your body releases adrenaline and catecholamine, both of which inhibit blood flow to your prefrontal cortex, the section of your brain responsible for higher thought and decision-making. Basically, your body is telling your brain to shut up, stop thinking and start running.

At the same time, your helpful brain imprints the memory and the response into your hippocampus (your memory bank) so it can access this pattern even faster in the future. While this function was designed so that our well-meaning brain could protect us from regular safety concerns, the modern side effect is that our bodies react to stressors much more quickly every time we encounter them, making it harder and harder to break the cycle.

Stress Makes You Sad

Cortisol disrupts the biological processes in your body, including the production of serotonin and dopamine. Both of these hormones serve to mellow you out and make you happy, neither of which is particularly useful during a stressful situation. Therefore, your body (in all its wisdom) suppresses them. While this is useful in the short term, long-term suppression of these hormones actually makes it more difficult for your brain to start producing them again. In the particular case of serotonin and dopamine, this means you'll be more vulnerable to depression, anxiety, insomnia and more.

Stress Makes You Sick

High levels of cortisol inhibit the actions of white blood cells–your body's natural defense system–leaving you defenseless against infection, less able to heal wounds and amplifying the symptoms of any pre-existing conditions.

Stress Makes You Sore

You may have heard that cortisol is used to treat inflammation (cortisone shots are administered to combat painful injuries), but it can also exacerbate inflammation. Why? Cortisol's main purpose is to heal inflammation, which is why it is released during times of stress and injury. However, long-term exposure to cortisol (which happens when you experience chronic stress) decreases your body's sensitivity to the hormone. When your body releases cortisol to fight an area of inflammation and your sensors are immune to it. The less effective the cortisol is, the more your body releases, and thus, your problem becomes chronic.

How to Diffuse Stress

When you've got an excess amount of stress stored up and are feeling overwhelmed, the first thing you have to do is to diffuse some of that stress in order to give your body a break and free your energy for other pursuits.

Traditionally stress has been viewed as a negative influence, but recent research has revealed that when people accepted their stress and acknowledged it for what it was (your body's way of providing you with the needed energy to overcome a frightening obstacle), the stress actually became an asset that helped them work more efficiently and become healthier.

So how can you use stress to your advantage? First,

you have to acknowledge that you are stressed, find out what is causing it and determine that you will use your stress to overcome the challenge at hand.

Easy, right? You'd think so, but most of us are so confined by our "roles" and our manners that we hardly ever tackle stress in an effective way, whether it be to let go of a project or to confront an enemy in the workplace. This causes our stress to multiply because we are unable to process and eliminate it.

Now, think of a monkey–how would a monkey handle his stress? He would either run away or attack, which is exactly what your body is telling you to do with all that adrenaline.

Traditionally, stressed office workers have been advised to take deep breaths, relax and ignore our bodily signals to tear apart our enemies, which is really, really bad advice. While it's healthy to relax at the end of the day, when there are no threats present and you're in a safe place, an immediate threat requires your body to respond with immediate action. If you override that impulse and choose not to act, your body will respond by sending even stronger signals, releasing more adrenaline into your blood stream and creating even more anxiety in the long run. Breathing your way through a crisis at work can be a recipe for disaster.

What your body is doing is giving you some options: fight, flight, tend or befriend. Trial and error will help determine which works best for you. Don't underestimate the power of a quick release of energy, whether that's in the form of exercise (which mimics fight or flight) or a brief heart-to-heart with a confidant (tend and befriend).

So the next time you're stressed, consider sneaking to the nearest hidden hallway for some burpies or sprints. This will tell your body that you've escaped the danger, and sends fresh, oxygenated blood to your brain, giving you an instant performance boost.

Be Your Own Boss

The one thing that all entrepreneurs love about what they do is that they are their own boss. Now, working for yourself is not for everyone, but the fear of disappointing others is often cited as one of the greatest sources of stress in the workplace. One recent study showed extremely high rates of depression in men who would much rather be home with their families or pursuing their own interests, but felt as though they had to spend upwards of 60 or 70 hours in the office just to fit in and maintain their status.

If you feel as though you are stuck in a rat race, there is one simple and proven method that you can use to get back on track: become your own boss. This entails setting your daily goals and the time at which you will walk away from your desk, and sticking to it. Having this schedule and a set of tasks that *you* determine will help you feel empowered and in charge of your working conditions, and avoid the depression and helplessness that often comes with feeling as though you are not in control of your life. The fact of the matter is that our work will continue forever, and working extra hours every day might feel productive at the time, but the fatigue and ennui will quickly start to wear on you, slowing you down in the log run.

By re-establishing a feeling of control you will be able to keep your stress hormones in check, prevent burnout, have a life, and also give the impression that you are confident and competent in your work.

Use Stress to Your Advantage

Once you've diffused the general feeling of malaise, you're ready to get back in touch with your stress and use it to your advantage, just as Mother Nature intended. I like to call this riding the rush.

Riding the rush can be a little tricky at first because it requires a lot of mental control as you rewrite the internal dialogue and meaning you have associated with the feelings of stress.

If, for instance, you are feeling scared before presenting to the board, remember that fear and excitement are basically the same thing on a chemical level: the only difference is the label you're assigning to it. So before heading into that boardroom, lock yourself in your office or a bathroom stall, assume the Victory or Wonder Woman pose and tell yourself how excited you are to be able to present to such a powerful group. Trust me, you'll feel the difference.

If you're an introvert or really nervous about a situation, don't hesitate to start this process earlier, because the more you practice confidence, optimism and excitement, the more your brain will become wired to think that way. If this becomes part of your neurological makeup, you will be greeting all challenges with excitement and joy, and that rush of adrenaline we call stress will become your new best friend.

Boredom and Stress

After one of my workshops on productivity and the

brain, one of the attendees came to me and broke down in tears. I was stunned that my simple keys to optimizing working efficiency had made such a powerful impact on her. As she composed herself, she began sharing how depressed she had been over the past few months, and how every single day at her comfortable, well-paid job had become a challenge. She had tried everything—more coffee, networking, therapy and regular exercise... but she just couldn't shake the loathing and malaise that permeated her working life.

As we talked more about her position, I was able to determine a handful of problems with her role: she wasn't being challenged, but even worse, was didn't have any deadlines or goals she was trying to achieve. Her job was simply to show up everyday and keep things running smoothly.

We all know stress is bad for our health, but what few people realize is that neurologically speaking, stress and lack of challenge can be deadly to our brains, our bodies, and our careers.

Our brains evolved to love learning and new experiences—two key factors that help us survive in the wild—which is why every time we experience something new or accomplish even the smallest of tasks we get a shot of the "feel good" neurotransmitter dopamine. When our brain is starved of dopamine, we can start feeling depressed, tired, mentally foggy and start gaining weight or feeling achy or twitchy all over.

Fortunately, dopamine is fairly easy to come by, and some simple adjustments can make anyone's working experience much more rewarding. If you have the time, try challenging yourself with a new project or meeting new people, but if you're already up to your ears in work, try breaking down your projects into checklists. Researchers have found that the simple act of checking off a box can release a burst of dopamine, as does having new experiences, such a trying new foods or going for a walk.

Looking at social media also provides the same burst of dopamine, but can often lead to another set of problems when the brain becomes dependent on microbursts of the neurotransmitter. This causes addiction-like symptoms, complete with emotional ups and downs and the guilt of having wasted an excessive amount of time on something that did not bear any fruit.

Speak the Truth

Life is too short to tell a lie, and if you do, your life will actually become even shorter. In line with not being nice all the time, it is also crucial that you learn how to express your true thoughts instead of hiding them or misrepresenting yourself in order to keep others happy.

Studies have shown that people who lie about what they think or feel leave an interaction with lower self-worth and self-esteem, both of which are linked to shorter life spans.

When you lie–even about something as simple as how you really feel about a decision made by management–cognitive dissonance grows in your brain. This internal conflict consumes energy and raises stress levels without resolving them, which can lead to long-term adrenal fatigue, depression and other problems.

111

The next time you're tempted to grit your teeth and say, "No, really, it's okay," think about what you're doing to your body, and instead say, "I disagree, but I can see where you're coming from and I defer to your judgment." Simply stating the truth while agreeing will protect your health, and will create an added dimension of authority and confidence.

For full disclosure, I should note that there is one upside to lying: chronic liars have 20 percent more white matter (which sends information from one part of the brain to another) than non-liars, giving them greater access to their whole brain. Tempting as this may be to grow your brain, lying can also cause a different kind of stress as you try to keep your ducks in order, so perhaps it's best to steer clear of lying in the office and pick up fiction writing on the side.

Move It, Lady

There are a number of challenges that can poison you in the workplace, but the truth is that the single most powerful demotivator is one that rests right under your butt.

Science has proven that the single most effective way to boost your competency and your confidence is to exercise on a regular basis. Studies have shown that sitting for extended periods of time decreases your blood circulation and is actually more harmful than smoking and drinking combined. Keeping your tush parked in your chair eight hours a day may make you a office hero, but do you really want to make that kind of sacrifice for the company?

When you sit in your chair, you're effectively blocking the blood flow to and from your brain, your extremities and your heart. This leaves you feeling less energized and lost in a thick mental fog.

Evolutionarily speaking, the human body was designed to walk up to 12 miles every day, so by sitting in our chairs, we are undermining our natural abilities, forcing our instincts into submission and putting a damper on our natural systems, thus sabotaging our ability to compete in the corporate jungle.

Even if it is just for short walks every hour, get up, move around the office and use this as an opportunity to increase and show off your physical strength, confidence and stamina.

Jump for Joy... and Smarts

Even mild exercise not only gets your blood moving and invigorates you, but also changes your hormonal and neurological profile.

Here's how it works. During exercise, your blood starts pumping and brings oxygen to all of your cells, organs and glands, which tells them to wake up and start producing the proper hormones to regulate your system.

Since your body is a large, thriving organism wherein all parts are interdependent, having an optimally performing pituitary gland (which controls your thyroid and your metabolism) will kick-start all of the connected systems, and will also help break up and expel the bad hormones that have been dumped in your body, including adrenaline and cortisol.

And the effect doesn't end there. Remember how your posture affects your hormones, and thereby affects your career success? Well, one of the easiest ways to improve your posture is to exercise. As you strengthen your core muscles, they will naturally pull you into alignment, giving you a strong, powerful presence on a physical and biological level.

But exercise doesn't just affect your presence. It can also give you a boost at work by stimulating the formation of new neurons, thus making you smarter and boosting your memory. While it is unclear why exercise increases memory, one theory suggests that back when we were hunting and gathering, our brains evolved to grow during exercise because this would help early humans navigate their complex environments and remember the way back to the caves.

One senior military general was facing a systemic energy crisis in his new office that was jeopardizing their success as a team. He took over the office from another leader and quickly discovered that people were unmotivated and insecure. They were in their chairs for eight hours a day, but so many of them associated their desks with stress that they were able to accomplish very little work in that time.

By simply encouraging his staff to go for two brief walks every day, he was able to break their stress habits, by helping them release the positive hormones that are created by exercise and by helping them break the negative associations they had all formed with their work environment. Within a few short weeks, absenteeism dropped and productivity increased as his employees were once again happy to come to work. They began associating those eight hours with positive encouragement and productivity rather than negative feedback and bottlenecks, which allowed them to concentrate on getting their work done, rather than keeping their heads down to avoid punishment.

Eat Yourself Smarter

Truth be told, this section should be called "Stop Eating Yourself Dumber." The more science learns about modern neurological maladies–including ADD, ADHD, mood disorders, forgetfulness and fatigue–the more it seems these are aggravated by what we eat. But before you go pumping yourself full of superfoods, take a moment to see if it's the un-super foods on your plate that might be causing your problems in the first place.

As a general rule of thumb, white foods should be consumed with moderation. This includes carbohydrates, sugar, high-fructose corn syrup and high-sugar fruits. A high supply of sugars in the blood raises insulin levels, which in turn block certain neurological cells related to memory and performance, all on top of raising your risk for diabetes. High-fructose corn syrup is a big culprit, but even products made out of refined flour can easily spike your blood sugar, causing the same decline in memory and mental performance. Consuming omega-3 fatty acids seems to counteract this effect to some extent, so luckily we have an antidote for when we fall off the sugar pony.

Artificial sweeteners are no better than their authentic cousins. These chemical compounds have been found to penetrate the brain easily, impede neurological function and cause brain fog, vision problems and migraines.

The trans fats found in fried foods and many processed snacks are another major culprit in

115

decreased mental ability. High consumption of trans fats interferes with your brain's ability to send signals, including those that tell you how full you feel, causing you to eat more than you need and leading to digestion and blood sugar problems. Luckily, the FDA banned artificially produced trans fats in processed foods while this book was being written, so this issue should be easy to avoid.

There are a number of foods that have been shown to boost brain power, whether by mitigating the effect that bad foods have on your brain, or simply because they are amazing.

Your brain is one of the biggest consumers of energy in the body, and therefore also releases the greatest amount of damaging oxidizing chemicals (free radicals), which get trapped in the fatty tissue surrounding your brain. Eating any antioxidant-rich foods (berries are a popular choice) will help give your brain a much-needed boost. Staying hydrated will also support optimal brain function and stave off headaches.

Curcumin, a component found in turmeric, is another powerful antioxidant and anti-inflammatory agent, and recent research has shown that it has the added benefit of providing substantial relief from menstrual cramps. Simply add a small piece of whole turmeric or a dash of the powdered stuff to your smoothie or pasta dish.

Seeds are great to provide your brain with the essential nutrients it craves. Pumpkin seeds are loaded with zinc, which boosts the immune system and the brain, and sunflower seeds are one of the best sources of magnesium. Magnesium stabilizes your mood, soothes your muscles and increases energy, and interestingly enough, it's also one of the most common deficiencies people have today.

Use Water to Focus

If you're having a hard time coming across as actively engaged, there is a small strategy you can use to become more powerful and focused in meetings: drink a big glass of water beforehand. Studies have shown that the urge to pee raised the level of focus and test scores in students. It's a great trick to help you get through those boring mandatory meetings.

Optimal hydration is also critical for decision-making. A common recommendation for fighter pilots before landing or participating in a demanding exercise is to hydrate and consume a small amount of glucose as that creates the ideal physical conditions for quick decision making.

Sleep Your Way to the Top

We love gossiping about how people sleep their way to the top, but the truth is, it's an extremely effective method to getting ahead. Best of all, you don't even have to climb into bed with anyone to reap the benefits.

Too many of us are hung up on being overachievers, often pushing ourselves to work late hours to prove our chops. But a lack of sleep–even an hour or two–carries devastating consequences for your mind and body.

Psychologically speaking, working late on a regular basis is bad for your stress levels, your self-esteem and your professional image. Internally, the constant drive to work late creates a loop of feeling as though you can't finish your tasks. This impacts your ego and your stress levels.

But more importantly, the inability to complete assigned projects during the regular 9-to-5 sends the message to your boss that you're inefficient, and may not be qualified for your job. If the reason you're working late is a legitimate one, make sure that those around you are aware of it to avoid tarnishing your image.

Image and ego aside, the biological consequences of working late are serious. Shift workers have higher rates of cancer and heart disease, and a lack of sleep has also been shown to cause neurological decay. Unfortunately, recent studies have shown that taking a power nap or sleeping in on the weekends to make up the deficit can't ameliorate the damage done to the sleep-deprived brain.

When you go to sleep, your body increases the flow of cerebrospinal fluids to the brain to wash out all of the toxins that have accumulated there over the course of the day. If your brain can't cleanse itself, the free radical toxins start piling up and damaging your brain. The science shows that the harder you work, the more sleep you need, so be sure to treat yourself to some quality zzzz's.

If the future threat of cognitive degeneration isn't enough to deter you from working long hours, know that melatonin, the hormone that regulates your sleep cycle, also regulates the formation of pigments in your skin. If you want to keep your skin looking healthy (and we know that a healthy appearance can have a positive impact on your career), be sure to keep a regular sleep schedule and avoid bright screens in the evening so as not to mess with your body's natural production of melatonin.

Now, even though it's not recommended to replace your regular night's sleep with naps, siestas do have their place. A NASA study has shown that a 40-minute nap restores alertness by 100 percent. Another study by napologist Sara Mednick showed that our senses become heightened after a midday snooze, allowing you to accomplish more in the second half of the day.

Recap: Work With Your Body

Pay Attention to Your Body
Your body is your most powerful ally. Learn to work with it and it will support you by telling the world what a powerful, strong creature you really are.

Don't Stress
Stress is the worst thing we can do to ourselves: it causes mental decline, early aging, illness, anxiety and depression. Recognize your stress, learn how to use it to your advantage and dispel any excess stress you have by exercising.

Speak Your Mind
Speaking your mind not only makes you appear more engaged and confident, it also changes your brain's perception of the importance of the situation and gets you more deeply involved in your work. Remember that not speaking your mind (or worse, lying) has a number of negative health effects.

Jump for Joy... and Smarts
Exercise is the single most important thing you can do to change your presence in the workplace, improve your cognitive function, energy and mood.

Eat Yourself Smarter
While there are no foods that will raise your IQ, certain foods can increase your cognitive performance, especially if you use them to replace the foods that have a negative impact on your mental functions.

Sleep Your Way to the Top

So many of us love to show off by working long hours and forsaking sleep to prove that we will finish the job no matter what it takes. Stop it! Not only does a lack of sleep wreak havoc on your body, mind and performance, it also sends a very clear message to the monkeys: this woman does not have what it takes to get her work done on time.

Trust Your Gut

There is a difference between gut and intuition: one refers to understanding the bones of a situation, the other to understanding the people. Women are naturally intuitive, so dive deep into understanding the business aspect so that your gut instincts can grow stronger. When you couple that with your natural intuition, you'll be unstoppable.

Rule # 5 Be a Pack Animal

Humans, especially female humans, have a fundamental, intrinsic sense of community and the need to belong. We thrive in groups, and often dedicate our time and energy to improving the conditions for everyone in the community in more subtle ways, which leads to us being overlooked and feeling frustrated and under appreciated. When that happens, we work even harder to stand out in a crowd, and slowly end up running ourselves ragged and burning out.

Teamwork is natural, but getting lost in the team isn't. Scientists strongly believe that our early ancestors worked in teams to surround large beasts and wear them down before sending in the strongest members of the clan for the kill. In other words, they coupled teamwork with exceptional personal performance.

The monkeys of the species learn this behavior through sports, which teach them to work well in groups and have no shame in seizing the moment to bring victory to their team. Women who have been taught to avoid the spotlight often believe that being competitive is a sign of bad manners and therefore avoid that kind of action. That leads us both to underperform in the eyes of the monkeys, and to judge them more harshly for their actions.

The chapter on Jungle Speak has taught you how to make yourself heard, but in your journey to get ahead you should also remember that you are expected to be a pack animal who understands how to bring about the greater good, as defined by the jungle rules.

When you play it right, your pack will support you in your endeavors, back you up when needed and provide you with valuable information and insight to accelerate your career.

In this chapter, you'll
• Learn which people you need to spend time with at work and which ones to avoid at all costs
• Create and nourish beneficial relationships that will boost your career
• Ensure that everyone in the office respects you without coming off as a brown-noser or Pollyanna
• Deal with office bullies and aggressive colleagues
• Find and capture the perfect mentor or sponsor

You Are Who You Run with

Choosing your pack is one of the most important decisions you will make in the office, as you will grow to resemble the four to six people with whom you spend the most time. It's easy to fall into the trap of choosing people who already resemble and support you, but in doing so you run a big risk of being surrounded by enablers who will inhibit your growth. Instead, find people who you admire and would like to grow into, who can teach you something and are more invested in seeing you grow out of your current role and into the next one, rather than those who want you to stay where you are.

You should also choose to spend time with people who have a fair amount of influence and respect in the company. In the wild, it is not unusual for the alpha females to have affairs with omega males, but they always do this in secret. When mingling with those whose influence on your career is neutral or negative, you'll want to make sure that you do it on the "down-low." If you truly find a gem worth your association, you can always indoctrinate that person into your pack and move him or her up the totem pole when the time is right.

Fitting in is Key

So what are companies looking for when they invite you into their jungles? Everyone has their own theories on this, but one company called Universum actually crunched the numbers and found the top five characteristics that companies seek: cultural fit, professionalism, high energy, intellectual curiosity and confidence.

Keep this in mind when you're applying to a job and trying to impress the recruiter. Hiring in this day and age is incredibly frustrating. HR is flooded with a heap of résumés that they must slog through before sitting through an endless series of awkward interviews and being disappointed by the few good candidates who choose to go to other companies.

Since cultural fit is the most commonly sought characteristic in job candidates, use this to your advance and forget worrying about whether or not you're the most qualified. The truth is that if the employer likes you, they will train you, so focus instead on making a friendly, cooperative and smart impression on the people who are hiring you, and worry later about proving your chops.

Choosing Your Pack

When you first enter the jungle, spend some time investigating the different creatures and being selective about the future members of your pack. The people you associate with can accelerate your career, but can also cause major setbacks if you're not careful. The jungle knows more than you think, so if you're seen as associating with the wrong people, your authority will diminish.

Start by getting to know the lay of the land and ask as many people as possible to share their experiences with you. The more you learn, the more you'll start to see the patterns of those who have the most influence. You want to be associated with those people, so invite them to lunch and ask them to share their experiences at the company, and their wisdom. Generally speaking, people will not turn down an invitation to speak highly of themselves.

As you get to know the other jungle inhabitants, you'll want to look for a handful of key factors: do they like their jobs? If so, great–will they push your work to higher levels? If not, they may be good sources of inside information. Have they been at the company longer than the average person? If so, what keeps them there and what are their secrets for getting ahead? Do they understand what exactly the boss and the company are looking for? If so, try to learn as much as possible from them.

The Pecking Order

Once you've gotten to know the key players in the office, it's time to start assembling your pack, which is made up of alphas, betas and omegas.

Your alphas are the supreme, rarely questioned leaders; your betas support the leaders and step in to support or replace them when they leave; and your omegas take care of the details and the heavy lifting that happens behind the scenes.

When you first start working, your pack will consist mostly of betas, but you'll also want to have one or two omegas in your circles, and hopefully, a couple of alphas. As you progress, you will know fewer omegas and betas as your inner circle becomes populated with alphas.

There are fundamental differences that set these three types of workers apart: alphas (whose ranks are mostly populated by monkeys) identify very strongly with the company and its goals, as well as their own personal goals within the greater framework. To an alpha, the company and his career are often inseparable. Keep this in mind when you're tempted to whine about work in front of your boss–he might take it as a personal insult.

Omegas are more interested in self-preservation, and while they are interested in the company, their primary objectives for being there are money and title, rather than feeling a strong identification with the company.

Omegas, on the other hand, are there because they need a job. They lack the insight and experience to find their true place in the jungle, but given time and mentoring, they are very capable of rising through the ranks.

So let's start with the omegas. You definitely want a handful of these in your pack because they can handle a lot of the small details, while also keeping you informed of the general vibe within the company. They are often the ones who bear the brunt of an angry beta, and best of all, they have something to prove. If they perceive you as a person of importance, it will be easy to work with them and get information from them in the long run.

But you shouldn't have too many omegas in your pack, as they are prone to codependence, and can easily become a distraction or give betas and alphas the impression that you identify with people in the lower rungs in the organization. Remember: in the corporate jungle, impressions are everything, and keeping up appearances is crucial. This doesn't mean that there is no place for sincere interactions, but nine times out of ten people will judge you on appearances before they get to know you.

The best way to maintain your relationship with the omegas is to offer them a professional umbrella, feedback and mentorship, as well as emotional support in the workplace. Omegas are primarily driven by relationships and immediate rewards, making them easy to please.

The bulk of your connections should be with the betas. The betas have been with the company long enough to know how things work, but aren't so high up the totem pole that they are beyond making connections with others in the jungle–namely you. Betas are ambitious and engaged in their work, and will be the ones who share the same values as you: wanting to work well and progress in the company, while not having it take over their whole lives.

The best way to maintain your beta relationships is by being irreplaceable, either as the gatekeeper to some knowledge or skill, or perhaps simply the iron-lipped person who can keep a secret or help them with a particular task. It is really important to be your authentic self and to know what you can offer without putting a drain on your personal resources.

Keep in mind that not all betas are created equally, so don't let their seniority in the company fool you. First of all, bad monkeys are smart and excellent at fooling people in order to get whatever they want, or get propelled to the top by their explosive temper.

Many managers don't want to deal with reprimanding ill-tempered monkeys, and so they simply let them slide through evaluations and pawn them off to other departments, even if that means giving them a promotion.

And finally, there are the alphas. Generally speaking, the alphas have two concerns: the well being of the company and their own personal well-being. Alphas tend to radiate confidence and excitement, which makes them very attractive. This is part of the reason why everyone wants to follow them. But when you're working with them, be sure that your body doesn't try to hijack you and throw you into a submissive position. If you find yourself gazing lovingly at your colleague, flipping your hair or leaning in just a little too much, check your signals and get back into your powerful poses. If not, you will catch their attention, but in the wrong way.

Nurturing Your Pack

Once you have a pack, it is absolutely crucial that you nurture it. But rather than blindly nurturing everyone who crosses your path, take a page out of Mother Nature's playbook and nurture only those who will pay you the greatest return. If you invest your energy into every jungle inhabitant, each bond you create will be a weak one. If, on the other hand, you carefully choose who receives your time and energy, you'll find that the relationships are so strong that even a rabid monkey can't break them.

One of the most important ways to nurture your pack is to create positive experiences when you are with them–if you're having a problem, limit your complaints to one or two sentences maximum and then focus on finding a solution. If they come to associate you with trouble and complaints, they will quickly dissociate themselves from you.

Getting regular face time with your pack is ideal, since it ignites our entire biology and forms deeper, more powerful bonds. However, when email and telephone are your only options, remember to be in touch at least once a month. No matter how evolved we are as humans, our attention spans are limited, and anything less than monthly check-ins will slowly begin to erode your relationship.

One excellent method for keeping in touch and accelerating your career, improving your health, and keeping your social network is to send five emails every week: one expressing gratitude, one summarizing your accomplishments to your boss, one connecting with a mentor, one making social plans, and one connecting with a loose tie connection.

The most well connected woman I've ever met is probably also the one with the smallest ego and lowest profile. This hospitality executive grew up in another country, and between culture shock and language barrier, she was actually quite shy at the beginning of her career. But she knew that if she wanted to succeed in a big city she would have to get connected, and so she sought out a mentor and learned how to network.

Every time she met someone new, she made a point of getting to know that person, and following up via email. When she came across something or someone that might be of interest to her new contact, she would send it straight over.

One day she received an invitation to provide feedback as a consulting gig for an international company through one of her connections. Because she had met and talked to so many people, she furnished a report so insightful that the general manager of the company—which turned out to be a major international hotel chain—phoned her directly and offered her a job.

Remember to nourish your network and treat the people you've chosen to have in it with respect. While you may not be able to see these people as much as you'd like, you can always make a small gesture. You never know how or when they may bring something amazing to your life.

Friends with Benefits

Many women make the mistake of offering favors in order to gain higher status or preferential treatment in the jungle. This kind of behavior takes many forms, from bringing food to running errands. But no matter what it looks like, this type of behavior can really damage your career.

In the mind of the monkey, offering gifts and favors only has two meanings: one is that you are submissive and asking for protection, and the other is a precursor to a personal relationship, often of intimate nature. While you may be interested in the latter (who isn't attracted to the alpha male in their lives?), both of these can have a negative influence on your career, and as much as possible, you should try to win your status through hard work and proving your worth.

Now, what if you're a helpful person who really

loves to do nice things for others? What if that is just your nature? Long answer short, you need to suppress that part of your personality as much as humanly possible–ultimately, everyone in the jungle should be fending for themselves, and if you're offering to do projects for others, you are basically calling out to the world, "Look at me! I'm an omega! Please take advantage of me!"

If you really can't control yourself, be sure to state the terms of these interactions, and make it clear that the only reason you are doing a favor is in exchange for a previous favor or in anticipation of a future return. For instance, you can say, "I really appreciate the help you offered me in A, and I can see that you're swamped with B. Why don't you let me help you finish that to repay you for the help you've given me in the past?"

What happens when you can't think of a way to fill in that sentence? Then don't do it! If a colleague truly needs help, he should ask you for it. If it's critical, always preface your offer of help with a statement that keeps him in his place, followed by an offer to help that's not phrased as a question. For instance, you could say, "I've noticed you were assigned a couple of extra projects. If you need the backup, I'd be happy to help with one."

Phrasing your offer to help as a question gives your coworker the decision-making power, and you should keep as much power to yourself as possible.

The Other Perk of the Network

Having a strong network is one of the most efficient ways to get anything done in business. Once you are well connected, you become a part of a tightly woven network of trust, and all other jungle inhabitants will want to contribute to your success because you contribute to theirs.

When you have a well-nurtured network–the kind where every piece of information, lead or new connection is something that proves useful to someone in your network–you become an indispensable part of people's lives, and they will begin sending resources your way. This is the ideal manifestation of the network, so remember to keep it tight enough so that you can be valuable to the people in your life.

Train the Monkeys

Nothing creates more lasting change in the jungle than a little bit of training and positive reinforcement. Remember, it's unhealthy and misguided to do favors for the monkeys as it shows submission and deprives you of authority. It is, however, completely indispensable to form a positive relationship with the monkeys wherein they come to associate you with positive emotions, a sense of accomplishment and a boost to their ego. Once you do this, you create a feedback loop that keeps them coming to you and asking for your time, keeping you in demand and in a position of power.

One savvy way to train the monkeys–especially those lower down on the food chain–is to keep snacks in your office drawer and make them available to stressed out, glucose-deprived monkeys. The boost in energy will cause them to associate you with positive feelings and increased productivity, as the sugar spike will often help them fix their own problems. The added perk is that people with low-blood sugar have poor impulse control, so you may hear a few juicy pieces of gossip that will help fill out your understanding of what's really going on in the jungle.

Treats aside, you must also make sure that interactions with you are positive. Nobody likes talking to people who are distracted, stressed, depressed or anxious, so be on your A-game when you meet with jungle dwellers.

Think ahead about all of the ways that you can make your colleagues' lives easier without coming off as submissive. One way you can do this is by simply collating or formatting any materials that you're sending out in a way that is easy to read and has clear directions on how to respond. The next time you have a number of questions, create a checklist or summary for the busy executive, rather than pinging him with ten separate emails.

Most people are inherently lazy, even if we're not. We enjoy it when others make our lives a little simpler, so whenever you're preparing to meet with an alpha or important beta, keep this in mind and prepare for the meeting to make it as stimulating and easy as possible.

Make Them Work for It

While no creature in the world will resist a free banana and pat on the head, the more neurologically complex creatures in this world–monkeys, humans, dolphins and mice–prefer a challenge, and if they aren't presented with one, they will often disengage and get wrapped up in other endeavors. Studies have found that three quarters of the American workforce feels unengaged in their jobs, which is a huge morale killer.

Try to keep this in your mind at all times when working with the monkeys. You already know that doing everything yourself is a disaster in the making, but the real question is how do you get others to do the work for you? The answer is simple: you have to use clear communications and create a challenge.

You already mastered the key components of clear communication in the previous chapter: be brief, assertive and share your thoughts simply and slowly in a low tone of voice, without adding too much additional information.

Here are some ways that you can create a challenge and motivate others to help you with your work. Or even better, to do it for you!

Pose a Question

Sometimes motivating the monkeys is as simple as rephrasing your request into a question that needs answering. Monkeys love showing off their cunning and intelligence, and when you give them a platform, they will often surprise you with their amazing results.

Remember to pose the question from a company angle rather than a personal one. Saying: "I would like to know" undermines your intelligence, whereas "It would be interesting to figure out why…" or "headquarters has asked us to find out what's happening with…" makes the request about the company rather than yourself, and creates a lot more interest and engagement from the group, as well as some authority for you as the representative of the company.

Create a Challenge

If the question was too subtle to motivate your monkeys, you'll need to step it up a notch by creating a challenge. Similar to a question, the challenge subtly implies that this project may be too difficult, or that there could be a big payoff for completing it.

Monkeys use this trick all the time to get others to do their work for them, usually employing the guise that they are training you or giving you a chance to show off your skills to higher authorities… right before they take credit for your work.

Create a Competition

Nothing sparks good work like a sense of competition, but studies have shown that prizes don't motivate people. Rather, people are motivated by proving themselves professionally and in comparison to others.

One way to do this is to frame this new project in comparison to a previous endeavor, challenging the group to outdo themselves. Alternatively, you can mention that another team is interested in this particular project, but that you believe this team has what it takes to put together the best report.

Be sure to infuse a little adrenaline into the

situation by framing it as time-sensitive or high-importance. When two teams are set to work on a project because the jungle needs answers as soon as possible, one of two things will happen: either the teams will begin working independently to show each other up, or they will start collaborating in order to come up with the best possible solution. Either way, you win!

Prick or Bolster Their Egos

Some monkeys are strongly motivated by challenges to their sense of pride and will try anything to try to prove your criticism wrong and impress you with their future work. Others find it extremely discouraging, and prefer to be motivated by compliments. Try to determine what motivates the monkeys in your team and act accordingly, but remember to proceed with caution. Once you've bruised someone's ego–the one thing that means more to them than anything else–it's hard to regain their trust.

Use the Monkey Smokescreen

While I can't stress enough the importance of being totally honest and faithful to yourself, it is sometimes useful, perhaps even necessary, to be a little dishonest with those around you.

Now, don't get me wrong: I'm not advocating that you go around lying about your qualifications or your personal achievements, but rather that you create a necessary buffer zone that protects you from the impact of the monkeys, whose immediacy of needs can often send you for a tailspin.

The monkey smokescreen is an excellent way to protect yourself, especially while you are still mastering the rules you've learned in this book. Here's how it works: when someone approaches you with a question or a request, tell them, "I am currently finishing up an important project, but I'll get it back to you as soon as I wrap this up."

When you do this, the monkeys will respect that you are working on another project, and will also come to understand that you are in control of your own time, which sends a strong signal of authority. It also prevents you from being too agreeable and taking on work that should be reserved for omegas.

During my time working in Intelligence, I learned about the monkey smokescreen. Because contract linguists and analysts enjoy a relatively private workspace, there was little information known about what we were working on at any given time. One day I was chatting with a colleague who was boosting his vocabulary and practicing his Chinese writing skills when a phone call came in. Our handlers had an important assignment that needed to be completed as soon as possible. My colleague graciously explained that he was swamped at the moment, but asked them to send the document over nonetheless, and that he would make it a top priority.

He must have heard my jaw drop as he hung up the phone, so he asked me if everything was all right. Naturally, I was totally shocked by his blatant lie, not to mention his willingness to turn down such a juicy assignment! He looked me in the eye and said, "You have to manage their expectations. Sure, I'm not busy today, but usually I am, and if they get accustomed to me jumping at their every command, they won't understand when I don't have time to do their work."

He started to turn back to his writing pad when another thought came to his mind. "Plus, you know what happens when people think you're in demand: they want you more." And it was true. His handlers practically had fight off others who wanted him on their teams. There was no doubt in my mind at the time that he was good, but in retrospect, I have to admit that he was truly great at his job.

Seek the Wisdom of Elders

While life in the jungle is cutthroat, you'll be happy to know that there are jungle elders–mentors and sponsors–who are not only happy to share their experiences wisdom with you, but to invest their energies into accelerating your career.

Both mentors and sponsors are senior or more experienced people in your company or network. The difference between the two is that a mentor acts more like a teacher–challenging and pushing you to develop your full potential–while a sponsor utilizes his own resources to further your career.

Finding a mentor is both easier and harder than you think, and it really begins with some reflection on your end to find out what it is you really want to learn. Like the monkeys, a mentor will be put off if you approach her with little more than a notion that you want to be amazing like her and learn everything she has to teach. It shows that you really don't understand where this person's strength and passion lies, and that you don't respect her time. If you did, you would have taken the time to find out what she does best, and how that works into your career plan.

Take a long hard look at your career, and then approach people strategically to help you overcome your areas of weakness. Getting general advice from Sheryl Sandberg (who admits that she is turned off by people asking her to be their mentor just because) is not nearly as valuable as learning how to crunch the numbers from a seasoned office manager who could do it in her sleep, just as asking your boss to mentor you in social media will be far less fruitful than asking the wiz kid who runs three websites on the side.

When you start meeting with your mentor, create a plan to track your progress and come prepared for every session. If you're not learning anything or progressing, it may be time to change your mentor, or at least the focus of your meetings. Remember, this is not a social visit: it is time that you and your mentor invest in your future.

Unlike a mentor–who coaches you through particular areas of development–a sponsor will leverage her own network to accelerate your career, whether it is by recommending you to sit on certain boards or introducing you to the right people. Generally speaking, a sponsor will choose you, but if you feel that you are ready to impress and have not been singled out, find someone who would make a great sponsor, and ask her to become your mentor. That way, you can show off your skills and hopefully convert your mentor into a sponsor.

I can't say enough about mentorship and its

many benefits–if it's done right. Over the years I have created and taken part in a number of mentorship programs, including one charity mentorship walk with more than 100 women from leading government organizations, nonprofits and Fortune 500 companies. For the women who pursued it earnestly, the rewards were immense.

Before I tell you about those, I'd like to tell you in which situations mentorship didn't work out. Having a powerful mentor was worthless for those who just did it because they wanted a connection, who didn't make it a priority, who thought their assigned mentor was not good or not famous enough and those who allowed their mentors' honest feedback to rub them the wrong way. If you end up in any of those situations, rethink why you're looking for a mentor in the first place.

That being said, I have witnessed hundreds of transformations of the years. One senior marketing executive whose market was dwindling really wanted to pursue her passion in food and arts, but didn't know where to start and didn't feel as though she had the chops. I introduced her to the head of a famous restaurant for a temporary gig, which blossomed into a mentoring relationship once this insanely busy CEO saw how talented the former marketer was in food. Her career soared, and she recently sent me a video clip of an appearance on national television.

Another woman I know wanted to take her small consulting company to the next level, and while she knew lots of women who were in the same field, she didn't want to grow like the others. She wanted to soar. She boldly approached a serial entrepreneur and leader of a major technology company. He had neither a deep understanding of her business or the technology that's used in her field, but he knew how to grow something from nothing, and before long, her company was steadily growing and she was presenting her workshops almost exclusively to Fortune 500 companies.

One of my own mentors wasn't sure what to do with her life: she was an extremely successful corporate executive at one of the top tech companies in the world, but it was costing her every last ounce of happiness and energy that she had. She decided to take a chance with one of the consultants who came to present at her company: she asked this consultant just how she did it. Before she knew it, she was tucked under the consultant's wings, learning the ins and outs of developing a platform, marketing herself and even how to run an international business that would allow her to travel around the world for work.

These are just a few of the many powerful examples I've seen of mentorship. Once you know who you are and what you want, start reaching out to people and asking them how they achieved their successes. Nothing excites people more than being respected and sought after. And best of all, I can't think of a single successful mentor-mentee relationship that didn't grow into a powerful friendship in the end, and as you know, having a close confidant and ally is priceless in the jungle.

Be the Warrior in the Pack

Being part of a pack doesn't mean you should become

one with it. You should always be a warrior: a woman who has her own intentions and goals, and puts her needs before those of others, though not at their expense. At the end of the day, if you're not taking care of yourself, no one else will do it for you.

When you first start acting in your own interest, it will feel as though you are being selfish. This is due to our upbringing and our communal instincts. Being your own warrior will free up an immense amount of time and energy as you stop worrying about everyone else's business. You will also notice that you are empowering those around you to be their best selves by no longer serving as their co-dependent enabler and by setting a positive role model of what you can achieve.

If you are unsure of whom you are and want to be, start by making a dream board, an inventory of your key values or list of your goals. Keep this nearby and review it every single day. Remember: your thoughts create your reality. The more you think about something, the more it becomes part of your cognitive framework, so fill your mental space with positive images. Not only will this help steer you to the right choices, but it will also navigate you away from poor choices. Whenever your thoughts go astray your brain will give you a nudge saying, "Hey, that wasn't in the plan!"

As you become more independent and self-centered (in a good way), there will be some people who may lash out at you. It's normal. The Chinese have a saying that says, "People hate becoming famous for the same reasons that pigs hate getting fat." Yes, when you become exceptional, people may target you, but consider that extra attention to be a validation of your efforts. Remind yourself that what you are doing is the right thing to do and that you are setting a good example. When necessary, take your critic aside and privately explain why you are focusing on yourself. Hopefully it will inspire that person to do the same.

Your Fellow Creatures

So you've met the monkeys, and you know about alphas, betas and omegas. Now it's time to go a level deeper and meet the other jungle creatures and figure out how to work with them.

There will be times when you come across creatures in the corporate jungle and wonder about their purpose. Remember that in this complex ecosystem we call the human psyche, everyone serves a purpose, even if it's not an obvious or a positive one, and that the people who challenge us often spur us to grow.

Monkeys

You already know that monkeys overrun the jungle, and while they are highly intelligent creatures, they are also self-centered, completely immersed in jungle culture and only looking to benefit themselves, leaving little space to consider the emotions of hardworking and equally competent human beings.

While many monkeys are men, it is also important to note that there are lots of women monkeys who can easily throw you for a loop. Because women are naturally inclined to look out for the good of the community, we hold a natural expectation that all women share the same values and goals that we do.

145

That disconnect is why we get so upset when we meet a female monkey in the flesh, and often accuse her of being cold, bitchy and selfish.

But isn't that an unfair standard for women? Just as we don't want to be judged for being too helpful or friendly, it's not right to judge a female monkey for being who she is. Keep this in mind if you ever have an encounter with a female monkey and are tempted to lash out at her for being curt with you. If you happen to butt heads, simply back off and approach her in a monkey-appropriate manner at a later date. Monkeys hate wasting time on talking about past issues, so simply show your deference and move on. Remember, with monkeys, it's all about the present and the future.

Termites

It is important to keep your ears to the trees and perform periodic spot-checks to make sure that termites aren't undermining your efforts in the workplace. You can spot termites by their apathetic and negative attitudes and their ability to wear away at the team's spirit and make projects less successful. While they may not be openly aggressive, termites will slowly corrode your team from within.

When you find yourself with a termite infestation, consider that they may be underutilized or disrespected in their current roles. Find out what motivates them, and reassign them so that their energies are put to good use. And if they happen to be unrepentant, chronic termites, do what good managers do, and find a way to have them transferred to another department or company.

Mosquitoes

It's amazing how many creatures feed off the jungle's abundance without really contributing anything positive to it. Mosquitoes are no exception: they thrive in workplaces where large projects, lack of oversight and lots of stale, corporate water create the perfect environment for them.

Mosquitoes can come in the form of managers or employees, but the one thing they share is that they will waste your time and energy with frivolous projects. If you have an infestation, the only way to deal with it is to become as unappealing as possible to them, either by using the smokescreen or refusing to engage. When they approach you with another time-wasting task, tell them you're in the middle of a specific project, and ask them to come back later.

And if all else fails, annoy them. There is nothing worse to a self-absorbed person who wants to talk about himself than having to hear about someone else, and before you know it, that mosquito will have buzzed off.

Spiders and Snakes

Spiders and snakes serve the same role in the jungle; only one of them should be your ally and the other your foe. Spiders, much like bugs, don't really contribute too much to the company, but they are incredibly useful in capturing and eating the other bugs.

Think of spiders as socially conscious team members who guard your time by deflecting unwelcome advances by other bugs that will eat up your energy. Because they are often invisible to the naked eye, spiders tend to have a lot of insider info and will be able to keep an eye on the jungle for you, even if they don't share everything they learn.

Just try not to walk into their webs and disrupt them, as spiders clearly define their own territories. Simply allow them to do what they do best and work with them. If you do, they will become great and useful allies.

Snakes also serve to get rid of some bugs, but have a much more malevolent appetite, and can often be seen munching on useful jungle creatures because they didn't have anything else to do at the time. If you suspect someone is a snake, make sure to keep your distance. Snakes are never up to any good, and you don't want to get bitten for being in the wrong place at the wrong time.

Mice

Ah, mice! Is there anything they can't do? Yes there is: they can't rule the jungle. But just because these hyper-intelligent creatures aren't born to rule doesn't mean that they can't help you.

Mice are extremely intelligent and productive, and if you train them and give them regular rewards, they can do a lot of your work for you, and keep an eye on things that are happening in the jungle.

Because worker mice are so ubiquitous and unthreatening, they can easily infiltrate other parts of the jungle and learn what is happening there. Just be sure to keep them busy and well fed, because if you don't, they will turn all of that productive energy into spinning their wheels, and can easily burn out or become frustrated at the lack of progress and rewards.

Elephants

These lumbering giants may not be useful in day-to-day operations, but elephants play a critical role in the jungle by sharing the insights and wisdom they have accumulated over the course of their long careers. You will meet few elephants in the wilds of the jungle, but when you do, try to learn as much from them as possible, and keep in favorable standing with them. They are well respected for their tenure, wisdom and understanding. Even if it seems as though they don't serve any practical purpose, know that simply being in their presence will deepen your understanding of the jungle, and remind you of its grandeur.

Birds

You know those people in the office who seem to soar in their careers, despite the fact that they are not doing that much? Those are your birds.

Naturally graceful and charming, they are beloved by all, even when they don't contribute as much as you may think they should. They help clean up a bug here and there, but much more importantly, they bring energy and joy into every situation, and that is really the greatest thing they can do.

Try to keep at least one bird nearby at all times to bring fresh energy and motivation to your team, and remember that they often have juicy pieces of information that can give you the leading edge.

Cats of Prey

These magnificent creatures are natural-born alphas and can seemingly turn on their charm in the blink of an eye. Big cats make life in the jungle appear easy and

149

natural–they leave other jungle creatures in awe of how they can stay at the top by making a limited number of very important kills.

The key lesson you can learn from cats of prey is to focus your energy on big, important goals that impress, rather than running yourself ragged trying to achieve perfection in all that you do.

While not all of us are born to be tigers or other mega predators, stay close to them and learn how to go after your goals with both grace and aggression. When you master that ability and couple it with your own innate skills, you will be unstoppable.

Crocodiles

These quiet but powerful creatures are the guardians of hidden domains, and will generally lay low until they are hungry. They are often perceived as unproductive, but that criticism isn't necessarily fair–they just manage their work in a different fashion than many other jungle animals. If you cross them at the wrong time or antagonize them, you could easily become their lunch.

If, however, you respect their work and working habits, you will gain the crocodiles' confidence, and will be able to move your projects through the pipelines a lot more quickly than others. If you have to work on a project with them, try luring them into your circle by offering them small, easily digested projects that create a positive association in dealing with you.

Recap: Be a Pack Animal

Having a Pack is Critical

Having a pack gives you a real advantage in the workplace: with it, you gain access to more people, power and information. Your pack can also serve as a support system to help you develop new skills and leverage them for maximum impact. Don't just seek out people who affirm your reality. Seek people who expand your professional horizons.

Be a Warrior

Remember that there is a difference between having a pack and becoming part of it. Know your own worth, values and convictions, and make your own path. You only serve your purpose in the jungle when you are unique, authentic and taking care of yourself.

Pick the Perfect Pack

The more time you spend with the people in your pack, the more closely you will come to resemble them, so be sure to choose the perfect combination of characters so that you can evolve and grow with them, rather than getting stuck in a rut, or devolving.

Train the Monkeys

Remember to make each encounter with you a positive one. Monkeys are creatures of habit and will seek out things that bring them pleasure, not things that bore, drain or stress them.

Seek the Wisdom of Elders

By connecting with jungle elders—either by asking one to be your mentor or by having one sponsor you—you can accelerate your career by getting great feedback, perspective and support. You don't have to go it alone, and while your pack can help you, a mentor or sponsor's influence will push you much further in a shorter period of time.

Rule # 6 Camouflage Wisely

Meeting a new person? You've got less than 30 seconds to convince them of your intelligence, authority, likability, and general worthiness of your attention. The pressure is on!

Women spend a lot of time focused on the details of their appearance, but the truth is that your new acquaintance takes only a quick glance before deciding what role you will play in your life. Like our body language and our speech, what we wear says a lot about us, but all too often, we allow it to say the wrong things. This chapter is all about developing your own unmistakable style that sets you apart from the crowd, without frightening the other jungle creatures or attracting predators.

In this chapter, you'll

- Learn to make a powerful first impression
- Avoid the biggest wardrobe mistakes women make in the workplace
- Use colors, scents and sound to manipulate your colleagues and boost your career
- Develop a signature marking that will set you apart in the jungle
- Use camouflage to distract your enemies

The Biggest Wardrobe Mistakes

At the end of the day we can only blame ourselves for sabotaging our careers by the way we dress. While there is plenty of advice on how to dress for the workplace, much of it is based on outdated etiquette books, rather than the hard science of how our appearance influences our presence in the workplace.

One of the most impressive women I've ever met was the Asian business manager for a major international law firm. From the moment she walked into the room you could sense her confidence, and it made her seem unstoppable. What was unusual about her is that she was very candid about how she had become the way she was: trial by fire.

As a young, ambitious woman, she had received a great deal of pushback from the men in her industry, and there were a lot of them. She learned very quickly that if she was going to succeed, she had to make herself invincible, which meant always being a step ahead, keeping her feelings in check even when she was antagonized, and always looking her best.

At our first meeting, she told me how she trained every new woman who entered the firm how to dress and act in the office. When these new employees started with the company, they were treated to a one-on-one consultation that taught the do's and don'ts of office fashion, followed by an office etiquette lesson. By creating this guidance, she was able to control how the monkeys in this male-dominated industry perceived the women, and was able to ensure that none of them had any generalized sexist ammunition that insulted the professionalism of the women in her office.

Here are the six biggest wardrobe mistakes a woman can make in the corporate jungle:

You Dress Too Provocatively
In one fascinating study, scientists scanned the male brain as it watched women in certain levels of undress. The women did not undress before them, but rather would appear wearing less and less clothing. There came a point where the male brain no longer registered the women as women, but began to light up in areas associated with viewing animals.

A little skin can make a big impression, but showing off too much will actually have your colleagues thinking of you in animal terms, which can seriously undermine your credibility.

You Dress Too Conservatively
While dressing too provocatively is a big no-no, it's wise to remember that on some level we're all hardwired for survival, and therefore, attracted to things that present an image of fertility. This involves being healthy, confident and well-kempt.

Look around your office and determine where the line between allure and dress code lies, and try to stick close to the former without overdoing it. As much as we like to claim that we are an evolved species, the truth is that we're often guided by our instincts, so make sure to use this to your advantage.

You Make Too Much Noise
Monkeys are single-minded creatures that show an

incredible drive toward their goals, but some are easily distracted by sounds and visual stimulus. If you're in the habit of wearing shiny jewelry that makes a lot of noise, you might inadvertently be setting yourself up to be ignored by important leaders in your company. Here's why: the constant noise and visual stimulation creates a distraction, but in order to stay focused on their goals, the monkeys begin to tune you out. Before you know it, you're no longer on their radar, even when you're not wearing distracting jewelry.

Don't get me wrong: bold, colorful and powerful statement pieces are more than acceptable in the jungle. In fact, I'd encourage them! Just don't put on anything that draws attention in a negative or distracting way.

You Change Too Much

Unless you work in fashion or a related field, don't change your wardrobe after every paycheck. It confuses the monkeys. Monkeys, as we know, are creatures of habit who become interested when there is something out of the ordinary, but can become subconsciously confused and irritated when it happens too frequently.

Fortunately they are not sensitive enough to pick up on small changes, but if your overall style or color palette changes drastically, it will be hard to miss and could put an immediate dent in your professional relationship as the monkey reassesses you and tries to figure out where to place you.

You Don't Use Color to Your Advantage

The perception of color and light are two things that

are fundamentally wired into the deepest regions of our brain and can influence us in powerful ways without us even knowing it. If you're constantly switching colors, the monkeys will eventually become numb to your presence, just as they might if you're making too much noise or being too flashy. Instead, save those big color changes for when you actually need to grab someone's attention–for instance, donning red in a big meeting.

You Smell

This isn't about body odor, but rather perfumes, which can have a powerful impact on the animals around you. It's hard to resist spraying a favorite scent every morning, but be careful not to overspray. You could easily irritate a sensitive monkey nearby, or worse, throw him for a loop when you've switched your scent.

Dress for Success

Dressing too provocatively is probably the biggest career blunder women make. In part, we can blame our biology and pop culture for making us want to show off more skin than we should, but even though this phenomenon is extremely common, it can have devastating effects on your career.

One set of research showed that women who wear too little are seen as less competent–regardless of how they perform–and that dressing in suggestive clothing can lower their salaries by a whopping 25 percent.

If you really want to be seen as attractive, stick to the real elements of attraction: health and confidence. All too often we get confused between dressing provocatively and presenting a healthy image because the women we are shown as examples in magazines and websites are 20 year old models posing as office workers. They are paid to be both healthy and sexy. For those of us who are just looking to get ahead in the corporate jungle, the former is enough.

Accessorize Wisely

Shiny, clinking accessories can wreak havoc on the monkey brain: they're disrupting, and while monkeys may enjoy a temporary flash here and there, the monkeys certainly don't appreciate you distracting them from their big goals every time you walk to the water cooler. Neurologically speaking, this makes *you* a disturbance, and our brains are designed to tune out those distractions.

But that doesn't mean you shouldn't accessorize! Having a single, powerful accessory can actually be extremely beneficial to your career, as this will become your trademark.

Whether it's an amazing set of eyeglass frames, a signature wardrobe combo, unusual shoes or another "pop" accessory, people will come to associate you with it, and you will have built your very own brand, making it easy for others to spot you in the corporate jungle.

You can even program your colleagues to associate completing assignments for you by subtly tapping or touching your accessory when discussing the matter. When done consistently, this is a great way to remind people to do certain things for you without having to say a word about it.

Making the Most of Your Makeup

Studies have shown that men preferred to associate with women who were moderately made-up. This is likely because that level of makeup mimics certain traits that are seen as highly fertile, such as glowing skin, rosy cheeks, big eyes and full, pouty lips. On top of that, you'll also want to conceal any under-eye circles, discolorations and blemishes you have on your skin, as these are all underlying signs of immune problems and weakness, which alert the other person's subconscious that you might be ill.

It may seem sexist that this book advocates women take extra steps to maintain a polished appearance in the workplace. Men are, of course, expected to maintain a well-groomed image as well. But the truth is that women are much more likely to show the status of our health in our skin, due in large part to greater fluctuations in hormones.

Women are also much more forgiving in our judgments of others, meaning that even an under-groomed male may receive the same level of respect from a female colleague as a perfectly groomed female. Nonetheless, no matter who you are, appearances matter, so you don't want to gamble with them.

Don't Let Shoes Cripple Your Success

We women are hardwired to look for stimulating colors, which is why shopping excites us in so many ways while it leaves our goal-seeking males frustrated and hopeless.

Shoes are such great example of this: while

women can spend hours searching for the perfect pair of shoes, men approach seeking their shoes in a much more practical fashion. To them, their goal is to find the perfect pair of shoes as soon as possible and get back to the hunt. This means they should be stable, comfortable and make them feel powerful.

Read that line twice: they should be stable, comfortable and make them feel powerful. When it comes to shoes, women are doing it all wrong. Many physicians have argued that wearing high heels not only imparts lasting damage on our feet structurally, but also pinches a lot of the nerves that can impair your mental functions.

Wearing high heels distorts the natural alignment of the spine and can compress the nerves, causing headaches, restricted blood flow and impaired thinking. Wearing heels can also affect your posture and balance, making you and you may come off as unsteady on your feet when it's vital to present an appearance of strength in the workplace.

If health reasons are not enough to convince you to stop wearing stilettos, know that one of the major complaints about women in the workplace is the constant clacking of their heels against hard floor surfaces. Again, if you're going to be distracting, you must always make sure it's in a positive fashion.

So trade in your ultra-high spikes for a sensible two- to three-inch heel and save your five-inchers for a date. You'll have all the confidence-enhancing benefits of a nice heel without detracting from your poise, and studies have shown that wearing heels firms up the pelvic floor, which will allow you to gain greater enjoyment from your romantic activities.

I once interviewed the general manager of the biggest luxury hotel in Beijing. Interviewing hotel general managers was always difficult because they were so good at presenting the company image and sticking to the official talking points that the resulting article could read just like the company's website. Eventually, though, he and I learned we had a shared passion and ended up casually chatting for two hours, during which I finally ended up asking him the question to which everyone was dying to know the answer: "Who are your worst customers?"

His answer surprised and amused me because it was both scathing and diplomatic at the same time. It turns out that this image-conscious hotel was, as you'd expect, really concerned with upholding appearances, and in his mind nothing undermined the hotel's and a person's appearance more than wearing the wrong shoes, be they dirty, too casual, or so high and uncomfortable that the wearer looked like a fool–or worse: a prostitute–while sporting them. The *nouveau riche* were particularly guilty of committing these kinds of fashion sins, and while he was happy to have their business, he did admit wanting to take them aside to talk to them about how bad they made themselves look by wearing flip flops or stripper heels in a five star hotel. Or anywhere else, for that matter.

Surprisingly, this was not the only high-ranking male executive who brought up the topic of shoes throughout my tenure. Perhaps it's one of the few fashion accessories that men pay attention to, but I can't count the number of times that people have cited shoes as their pet peeve in the office, whether it was because they were worn out, noisy, or just making the wearer look like a drunken giraffe or a brooding teen.

Men may not understand the nuances of shoes or why we spend so much time shopping for them, but they do know when a shoe isn't working. Blame this on their keen ability to determine the hierarchy in the workplace based on your posture and presence. If your shoe isn't empowering you, change it! It will give you an instant boost in appearance, as well as an opportunity to enjoy more shoe shopping.

The Smell of Success

One of the most powerful influencers in our everyday lives is our sense of smell. As cave people, we relied on it the same way that modern day dogs do: to find food and mates, determine risks, mark our territory and just get a general sense of what's going on. As one of my friends once remarked, "Dogs sniff each other's butts. [That's how] they know what's up!"

Scents help us subconsciously determine relationships, and changing your scent frequently may subconsciously upset those around you as their brains try to figure out what's going on.

So instead of changing scents often, use fragrance as a powerful tool that can get you noticed when necessary. Always keep in mind that being excessively scented will irritate those around you, thus undermining your efforts.

You should also consider employing trigger scents to meet your goals. The olfactory system is the part of the brain that has the most powerful link to the limbic structures that process emotion and associative learning. This makes it the perfect channel to lure someone to your team and to train them to stay there. If people come to associate a positive environment (meetings in your office) with positive odors (which you've created) and with positive outcomes, they will automatically have more positive reactions whenever that scent is involved.

While some studies suggest that the response to scents is culturally dependent (such as British people of an older generation despising spearmint because of its use in medicine), there are contrary studies that prove that certain fragrances have a positive effect on stress and productivity, no matter where they are applied. This is likely due to the phytonutrients associated with particular food groups and their scents. Some of these universal scent influencers are outlined in the table below:

Fragrances and their Effect on Performance	
Motivational: increases energy, stamina and mental clarity, even after periods of exhaustion	Lemon, eucalyptus, mint, ginger, tangerine
Soothing: lowers blood pressure and stress hormones, which can promote rest as well as better concentration	Frankincense, myrrh, cedar, vanilla, hyacinth, almond, lavender

Take a cue from retailers and add a little "environmental fragrance" to your office space. Retailers may see more than a 50 percent increases in sales when they start using fragrances in the right environment. One study, which pumped a casino full of floral scents for one weekend, saw a 45 percent increase in money spent. So keep this in mind if you're having a meeting to discuss a budget increase or raise with your boss.

Just be sure that the scent you use is not out of place, like the fragrance of freshly-baked cookies in a bus stop or restroom. When we smell things that don't fit into our environments, our primate brains become suspicious and apprehensive, meaning you're more likely to be denied or even antagonized because you're associated with that discordant environment.

The Problem with Perfume

Perfume comes with two big downsides: one, many people don't like the smell of some popular perfumes (and shampoos, so choose some that smell more natural), but they can also cover up some of the biological markers that let jungle dwellers understand your role.

A general rule of thumb is to spray lightly, but also to stick to fragrances that include natural notes. Doing so might actually activate some of the positive responses we talked about previously, and will at least do less harm than overbearing fragrances.

Not overloading your senses with scents also has an additional perk: our ability to smell is directly related to our levels of happiness and security, since our primate brains rely on the sense of smell to assess what's happening around us. Constantly bombarding our surroundings with different fragrances (dryer sheets, shampoo, body wash, cosmetics, cleaning products, room spray, etc.) can actually dull our olfactory senses and impair our sense of smell, a phenomenon that is seen in psychological diseases as depression and schizophrenia.

Spray on Some Confidence

While there are scents that have profound effects on us for biological reasons, evidence has shown that scents also have a powerful effect on us for psychological reasons. One British study had men spritz themselves with body spray before recording videos of themselves, and then had women rate the men in the videos on attractiveness.

The results? Overwhelmingly, the men wearing body spray were perceived as more attractive, even though previous screenings had ranked them on par with all the others. The difference? The freshly-fragranced men felt more confident, which changed their expressions and their body language, and actually *made* them more confident. The women perceived this visually, and rated them as more attractive.

Believe it or not, I actually know a tech entrepreneur who used this trick to boost the confidence of her delivery team, most of who were young and had never even talked to foreigners, which was their main customer base. Therefore, the idea of walking up to their doors was a little intimidating.

Deodorants are not very common in China, both because the Chinese produce less offensive body odors as compared to their western counterparts and because the body wash industry has yet to start marketing. To these young men, deodorant was a very exclusive western thing. Once these men began using deodorants, they actually started to feel more confident and better entitled to work with foreigners. The difference in their confidence was remarkable.

Something powerful happens to us when we groom ourselves. The next time you're considering a new lipstick, change your inner narrative to tell yourself that it's a business investment rather an impulse buy. That way, every time you reach for that tube, you'll get an instant confidence boost as you apply a fresh layer of success.

Using Colors to Get Ahead

Colors have primal effect on our brain because they are linked to our desire to obtain nourishing foods, which makes them a great tool to use to manipulate ourselves and those around us.

Keep in mind that you'll want to use this technique in moderation. As you know, monkeys and most other human beings are very sensitive to changes in their environment. If you are constantly mixing things up, the monkeys will eventually have to tune you out in order to protect their focus. The females of the species are biologically less inclined to become upset by this, and may actually be more intrigued. Just monitor the situation closely so that you can use the tool most effectively without overusing it.

At this point you may be starting to get a little skeptical about manipulating those around you, and you'll be relieved to know that it's actually very common in nature to do so: children and animals change their tone of voice in order to attract the attention of caregivers, and animals and humans change their posture (and scents) to elicit a response from other humans. So rest assured that what you're doing is fundamentally natural.

Colors and Their Neurological Impact

Colors have a powerful impact on our brains, and can stimulate everything from hunger to sadness. This is rooted in our age-old drive to look for edibles to sustain life as cave people. Fast food companies are hands-down the best at using both color and scents to manipulate customers: yellow, red and orange are colors that are associated with highly nutritious foods, which immediately tell our primate brains that we should dig in and store some calories for the harsh winter ahead.

Color can have a powerful impact on performance. If you have a particular task to accomplish, consider using some of the colors below to help you along the way.

Red stimulates the adrenals and neurons, the heart and respiratory system.	
Positive Effect	**Negative Effect**
Invigorating. Studies show men feel more affectionate toward women in red.	Can be overly stimulating and cause stress, frustration and anxiety.

Yellow triggers serotonin release in the brain, which leads to happiness and better memory. Speeds up metabolism and boosts the appetite.

Positive Effect	Negative Effect
Enhances memory and gives the brain a wake-up call.	Can be overly stimulating and excessive exposure may cause people to lose their temper.

Black absorbs energy and invokes a sense of power, authority, knowledge and intelligence.

Positive Effect	Negative Effect
Draws the eye. Black items appear more valuable and people will pay higher prices for them.	Excessive use can cause aggression. Hockey players who wear black jerseys are statistically more likely to be penalized for fouls.

Green soothes and calms the body (especially after trauma) and eases eyestrain.

Positive Effect	Negative Effect
People working in green offices reported higher workplace satisfaction. Shops report increased spending. Dark green is more effective on men.	Excessive use of green may kill productivity in the office.

White can be soothing in some settings, excessive use can overstimulate the eyes and brain.

Positive Effect	Negative Effect
Helps ease anxiety and can reduce stress and body tremors.	Heavy use of white can be tiring, and makes people feel cold.

Blue soothes nerves and suppresses the appetite.

Positive Effect	Negative Effect
Increases creativity. Makes items appear lighter.	Overexposure may lead to depression.

So the question is, how can you use colors to improve your work performance and influence other people? To boost your performance (and that of your team), you can use colored clothing, backdrops and PowerPoint slides to entice the proper effect.

Your afternoon cup of coffee will be a lot more powerful if served in a yellow cup, for instance, or you might have your team switch their computer backgrounds to blue during a creative brainstorming session.

Using color to get noticed works the same way. If you need to be noticed and respected, wear a black suit or dress, but offset it with a colorful necklace or white strand of pearls so that you don't seem too aggressive or intimidating. If you want to get noticed, wear a red sweater. This will be particularly powerful if you happen to be ovulating. If you're facing a tough board meeting where you're likely to get run through the ringer for your team's underperformance, sporting some green might take the edge off. And while some people can't wear vibrant yellow easily or well, try integrating that color into an afternoon meeting's presentation slides where people are more concerned with napping than paying attention to your findings.

Beware of Tones

If you're using particular colors in your wardrobe as means to an end, beware. There is one aspect of color that is often overlooked, and can undermine your efforts by making you appear pale and sickly, a major turnoff in the jungle!

Tone is the hue that a color carries. If you are wearing the wrong tone, you can appear washed-out and sickly, so be sure to consider tone of your clothing with as much thought as you do the cut and color.

There are warm tones and cool tones that exist both in clothing as well as in your skin. *Color Me Beautiful* is the classic book that defines the four "seasons" and teaches you which colors and tones best flatter your complexion.

Recap: Camouflage Wisely

Dress Appropriately

As the (stupid) old saying about skirts and essays goes, both should be long enough to cover the subject and short enough to be interesting. Dress according to the workplace norm, plus a little something extra to stand out, and above all, avoid dressing too provocatively, as that could cause irreparable damage to your career.

Avoid the Bling

While having signature jewelry pieces can be an asset in helping you stand out in a crowd, switching up styles too much causes confusion and anxiety, and wearing flashy or loud accessories can distract the monkeys and rob them of their energy and focus. Doing this once in a while is acceptable, but if you make a habit of it, your fellow jungle dwellers will soon start tuning you out.

Buy Shoes Like a Man

Wearing high heels may give you a boost of confidence, but heels that are too high can affect your posture, causing physical damage to your feet, spine and brain, and career damage as you hunch over and give a less-than-powerful impression. Unless you can rock heels like a runway model, stick to more sensible shoes.

Use Scents Wisely

There are many powerful fragrances that can be used to manipulate your colleagues and yourself into better performance and higher appraisals, but spraying too much can cause agitation in your colleagues, so do yourself a favor and let soft scents and pheromones do the talking for you.

Pay Attention to Colors and Tones

Colors can have a powerful impact on yourself and your team, so use them carefully and with intention. Tones are important too, as the wrong ones can wash you out visually and make you appear sickly, a no-no in the corporate jungle.

Rule # 7 Practice Black Magic

This is where the real fun begins. You have mastered control over yourself and learned how your presence can influence others. Now the time has come to learn a little bit of black magic to give your career a kick-start and get you out of tricky situations.

Please keep in mind that these are not tricks. A "trick" implies a sleight of hand, something sneaky and inappropriate; these black magic solutions are scientifically proven methods designed by Mother Nature herself to help you get ahead at work. Who are we to question her wisdom?

The only reason these skills may feel like tricks is they aren't natural *to you*, and they will require you to be smart and a little cunning, which may be under-utilized capabilities within your skill set.

A number of elements of this chapter have been covered previously in this book, but in this chapter you will learn how to put them into action in a way that brings quick, powerful and immediate results that lead to more power, respect and success in the office.

But beware! As you read through these strategies, you're likely to discover that certain people may have been using a number of these tactics on you. If that's the case, don't get angry; get even! Remember, all's fair in love and the jungle.

In this chapter, you'll
• Master the secret skills you need to build a loyal following and gain respect in the corporate jungle
• Learn the ins and outs of psychological conditioning
• Organize your space for success and power
• Program people to think highly of you
• Pick up phrases that will get you whatever you want
• Defend yourself against common tactics used to disarm you in the workplace

Create the Perfect Environment

Organize Your Office for Success

Sometimes where you sit can be just as important as how you sit, so spend some time to figure out the most advantageous positions for you.

One of the most important factors is the direction in which you are facing: you'll always want to sit in such a way that you are facing the door, or if you're in an open space, facing the direction of your supervisor.

As much as possible, try to avoid turning your back to a door or busy area. This is considered bad *Feng Shui*, but even more importantly, it wreaks havoc on your body, as it is a position that requires constant vigilance to threat, which can become exhausting.

If Lady Luck has been cruel and you end up sitting in the middle of a high-flow area, you can protect yourself by blocking your area with some plants or bookshelves to keep out some of that energy and those distractions.

But if you're stuck, make sure you make the most of your space and really spread out and take up more room. The smaller you are, the less authoritative you seem, and the less space you're perceived as needing, meaning it will be taken away from you.

If you're so productive that your work is spilling over into neighboring territories and that your desk is constantly buzzing with productive work meetings, your boss will start thinking of ways to give you more space. Just try to be relatively neat so that you don't look like a slob as opposed to a productive powerhouse.

Now let's assume that you have an office, or at

least a corner desk. Remember, you want to be facing the other people in the workplace jungle. Whoever sits behind the desk holds the power, and that is why you should stay away from meeting in the office of someone who ranks below you. If it becomes necessary to do so, consider remaining standing to ensure that you retain your authority, but don't be above sitting down if the situation calls for it, like during a private discussion of personal matters.

Back in your office, remember that sitting behind your desk sends a powerful message of authority, which can be amplified by securing a high-backed chair to make you look bigger and more powerful than you actually are. If, however, you want to create a deeper bond with someone, moving out from behind your desk during the discussion is one of the most powerful gestures you can make.

Be a Breath of Fresh Air

Most office lack adequate ventilation and many have mold growing in the air systems. Add to that the electromagnetic radiation you're picking up from all those computers and the bright lights that can lead to headache, fatigue, stress, anxiety, cardiovascular disease and insomnia, and it becomes clear why so many people feel like crap while in the office.

But don't despair! This is an opportunity in the making. By creating an inviting and healthy space, people will be drawn to you, even if they can't put their fingers on why they feel so great around you. Your presence will make them feel happier and healthier, and before you know it, everyone will be eager to work with you.

One simple way to do this is to buy some floor lamps and change up the lighting in your room. Strong overhead lighting amplifies emotions and makes situations more stressful. Naturally placed lighting (like floor lamps or softer lights) actually softens people's feelings and expressions and make them appear healthier, so you get the double benefit of having a more relaxed meeting environment and looking better yourself.

Salt crystal lamps are another great tool. They release negative ions that bind with pollution in the air and cause it to drop, creating cleaner air. Plants in general create a more welcoming environment, but succulents and cacti actually attract the electromagnetic radiation your electronics generate, and can ease eyestrain as well as headaches.

If the air in your office is particularly dry or dank, consider adding a humidifier or a purifier, and don't hesitate to use a drop or two of essential oils in the air. Just don't use too much. The key is to implement all of these strategies without anyone consciously recognizing them.

Create Instant Rapport

Bond Over Something Hot

If you need to break the ice with someone, buy or fetch him a hot drink. Studies have shown that when you talk to someone while he is eating or drinking something warm or hot, he comes to associate you with more warm and positive emotions. This works even if the other person only holds your hot beverage for a moment–for instance, while you appear to be juggling a stack of papers or taking off your coat.

When possible (and appropriate), also use the coffee handoff as an excuse to touch your target in a natural way. Makeup and perfume companies have known for a long time–and science has confirmed–that direct contact makes you seem more approachable and trustworthy.

Mirror Behaviors

We know that monkeys are creatures of habit and that they prefer a certain amount of consistency in their lives. This is why one of the most powerful things you can do to persuade a monkey to join your following (or at least to let you approach) is to mirror his body language.

Researchers at New York University found that when you mirror a person's body language, he or she immediately develops positive feelings toward you.

Do Some Snooping

Another black magic tool for bonding with someone is to talk about the things that they are interested in or hold in high esteem. This reaffirms that person's beliefs and also makes you a more attractive person to work with, since most people are drawn to those who share similar values. The key is that your subject can't know that you know that this is something he likes. It has to seem completely natural.

Try noticing the books in your target's office or items on his desk and bring related topics up during your next conversation. Remember, subtlety is the key.

If this person's interests are sorely outside of your

intellectual comfort zone or area of interest, swap the strategy and ask him a question related to the subject instead, and then listen with rapture as he dazzles you with his deep and profound knowledge.

Master Psychological Conditioning

Ivan Pavlov was a Russian physiologist most famous for his research in training dogs to drool on command. You can condition your fellow jungle-dwellers to do the same.

You've read this lesson before: unless you are dealing with an aggravated situation, you should ensure that all of your interactions in the jungle are positive and productive. That means no whining, no complaining and no excuses.

The reasoning behind this is very simple: humans are instinctively drawn to people with power and energy, and deep down in our primate brains we are drawn to people who exude happiness and health. If you are always complaining about something, you may win people's sympathy and the ear of the office gossips, but you will never win their respect.

Some of the great ways that you can condition people around you is to always greet them with welcoming, open body language (but not a big smile), to nod gently and insightfully while they are talking to indicate respect without showing approval, and to talk to them in a way that shows you are engaged.

When someone approaches you with a brilliant plan say, "You know, that's a really good idea," with a straight face, neutral tone and delayed smile. It makes you seem more sincere and powerful than bubbling over with enthusiasm.

Appealing to someone's ego is a very powerful way to win their affection, although if you don't do this subtly, they will sense that you want something and instinctively push you away.

Find ways to rephrase things that your subject has said so as to make them seem more intelligent or powerful than they really are. When you do this well, you'll give that person an instant serotonin rush (that they directly associate with you) and voila! they begin to form a powerfully positive association with you.

If you're having a hard time starting this, you can use an old Hollywood trick an actress friend taught me: while you're looking at someone, imagine yourself in a warm embrace with him or her. This can be platonic or sexual—that's totally up to you. Doing so relaxes your face and eyes, which makes you appear more genuine and caring. Biologically we already know that this trick actually releases the bonding hormone oxytocin, and the combination of the two will make a powerful impact.

When you think about conditioning, think about what appeals to our primal instincts. Any appeal to those instincts is not only difficult to detect, but will also be really powerful and hard to undo.

Reward Good Behavior
You can easily use positive affirmations, slight nods and the occasional smiles to enforce positive behaviors as they are happening, and also use engaged body language to show that you are really interested in what someone is doing. But also remember to use negative body language to discourage people from doing certain

things, like going on and on, making dumb comments or even to sway the room while someone is presenting a competing proposal. This is a great way of controlling the situation without being pegged as being bossy.

If you want to use negative conditioning, reflect back on some of that negative body language we talked about earlier and use it on occasion. This includes learning back, crossing your arms, furrowing your brow and looking tired.

It's really that simple to send a negative message and discourage certain behaviors, and because it's so simple, you should also be wary of other people using it in your presence. If you catch someone in the act, disarm them by changing the pace, the situation or maybe using some other poses to change the dynamic of the room.

One thing to keep in mind is that negative or positive body language doesn't always mean what it appears to: it could easily be the result of bad habits, bad posture or a bad night's sleep. You already know that women in particular are trained by society to have overly positive or demure body language, thus secretly undermining their workplace success. Keep this in mind whenever you are about to judge anyone, and whatever you do, don't stress about it. Even if someone doesn't like you, that doesn't mean that you can't work together in the jungle.

Use the Active and Passive Voices
We've talked about the dangers of being perceived as an animal in how we dress, but there is a similar

linguistic danger that lurks in our vocabularies: the passive voice. Our cultural upbringing has taught us to attribute actions to the group, to avoid taking credit for everything and to keep a low profile. You've already learned that this is the ticket to staying exactly where you are, as you give away the prestige and the rewards for all of your hard work.

To fix this, try the following swap: instead of saying, "The report is done," say "I finished the report." Also beware of using "we" when "I" would be more correct or more advantageous, and always speak in the active voice, unless you are in trouble. Speaking in the passive voice actually de-humanizes you and takes your responsibility and contributions away from the situation.

Keep this in mind if you need to undermine an enemy in the jungle. When you use the passive voice to talk about them, it gives the impression that they are less engaged in their work, and that will lower their significance in your boss's mind.

Say Thank You

There is a magic formula that makes you instantly appear more intelligent to your boss: whenever he gives you feedback or criticism, immediately say, "thank you." This has been proven to make you appear more competent in his eyes because you are agreeing with his truth and acknowledging his superior position and intelligence. This will work wonders no matter what he has just shared with you.

If you are in trouble, follow the protocol you learned in Jungle Speak and avoid any justification; instead promise to remedy the situation immediately, and do so. Don't hesitate to ask the right questions while you're belly up. Being in a submissive position is the perfect time to get more detailed feedback and advice, as the monkey sees this as an educational moment. If you come back later, chances are he will be busy with something else and you will end up reminding him that you screwed up in the first place.

Be a Mystery

There are many good reasons for not over-sharing in the office: you may bore your colleagues, or reveal information about your personal life that doesn't sit well with others, or lowers their impressions of you.

Another reason not to share is because you don't want to become too personal with anyone in the office–offering up too much information is always considered a sign of weakness and should be used strategically, if at all. Even sharing in small ways can snowball into the desire to share as your community-building instincts overwhelm your better senses.

But the biggest reason not to over-share in the workplace is that by remaining a mystery, others will remain curious about you and will be more inclined to offer greater rewards in exchange for you sharing certain information, whether it's related to work or not.

Think of this as a simple example of supply and demand: when you are constantly sharing with others in the workplace, your precious information loses its value. When, however, you remain somewhat of a mystery, the curious monkeys will be much more inclined to work with you in order to discover who you really are.

Appear Smarter

Take Notes

Perhaps this stems from our inner primate's fascination with the written word, but studies have shown that people who take notes appear to be more organized, competent and intelligent. And, best of all, the mere act of scribbling in a notebook does the trick! Don't forget to balance taking notes with your posture and your engagement so that you're not sending any passive or evasive messages.

File It Away

Taking notes makes you appear more intelligent but so does having a filing system for them. From a psychological perspective, people are attracted to information that is confidential or hidden, so keeping your notes in manila folders will create the illusion of greater authority, while also throwing up the smokescreen (or not, you may actually be very busy!) that you have a lot of things going on. Furthermore, handing over a file in a manila folder makes the document appear more substantial, and therefore, more impressive and important.

Attribute the Experts

One of the most common communication mistakes that women make is belittling their own opinions by adding phrases such as, "I think," "I may be wrong, but," etc. Once you've eliminated these junk phrases, there is another powerful way to boost your language in the corporate jungle: by attributing the experts. This creates social proof of what you're saying, and will override their desire to seek external validation.

While you don't want to overuse it, this tip can be a really powerful tool, as many monkeys are liable to think of women as less competent and intelligent (not because they don't like women, but because of what they've been taught and how we've been presenting ourselves), and a monkey raised in the wrong culture may feel inclined to seek a second opinion after speaking to you while he would happily take that same statement at face value from a man.

If you happen to be working with one of these specimens, save them the trouble of second-guessing you by attributing your findings to someone else– scientists, politicians or researchers. If you can, be specific, but know that often just hearing that you got the information from a credible source is enough for them. After your brilliant findings have proven to be true several times, you will become a trustworthy source of information and can slowly begin to drop the attribution.

Swear Like a (Nice) Sailor

A few years back, a study indicated that people who curse were perceived as more honest and trustworthy than those who did not. If you're rolling your eyes at this idea, you're not alone. This notion has been challenged, but from personal experience I can tell you that an effectively placed and sincere swear can increase your authenticity.

That being said, there are some powerful effects that come from occasional swearing, the first being that occasional swears from non-swearers make that person seem more authentic and engaged in the situation, and hence, more trustworthy.

Swearing also makes you feel and appear more in control, in large part because you're moving away from the tendency to brush over things and humor those who have upset you; instead, you're marking and defending your territory.

Most interestingly, however, is that swearing can give you an additional boost of adrenaline. Swearing activates your fight or flight response, making you more focused, more decisive and less sensitive to pain as adrenaline's analgesic effects kick in. If you ever need to rally yourself and your team to push through a tough time, a couple of well-placed curse words may do the trick.

Choose the Left Seat

One of the fortunate side effects of your brain's left/right wiring is that you can manipulate how much of your message your boss hears simply by choosing the proper seat in the office. When you sit across from your boss, choose the seat to your left. This will place you in the right side of the monkey's visual field, making him three times more likely to hear and remember what you're saying.

Use this when you want to be heard, and make sure you sit on the right side on a day when you'd prefer to have the spotlight pointing in another direction.

Wear Makeup

We've covered a handful of tips that show how awareness of and mastery over your body can accelerate your success in the corporate jungle, including paying attention to your stress level, speaking at a lower tone and even strategically engaging the monkeys around your ovulation in order to mesmerize them with your presence.

Another way to use your body to get ahead is to apply makeup before big presentations. This doesn't need to be anything fancy, but just enough to get noticed, as studies have shown that women who wear makeup are considered more intelligent and competent by both men and women, and believe it or not, even by preschoolers.

Wear Red During Your Review

While wearing red has been shown to make women more endearing to men, it also has the pleasant side effect of making you appear more successful at anything you are doing. Studies have shown that athletes who wear red are ranked higher against their fellow competitors, even when their performance is less impressive.

Practice Personal PR

Remember how the monkey brain can hold very little information at any time and is always being dazzled and swept away by another idea? Keep this in mind when you want the monkeys to remember something about you.

As much as possible, preface your statements with the tasks you've recently accomplished, maybe drop a line about the great job you and your team did and *then* lead into your true purpose for the meeting. You may have to devise some good reasons to see your boss and supervisor, and when you do, always keep in mind that you want them to leave the conversation feeling better than before your meeting began.

Consider phrases like this: "Hey Monkey, I just wrapped up the banana report and we got really great client feedback. I'm now moving on to the pineapple case, and since you really know the field, I was hoping you could give this memo a once-over and let me know what you think." Keep the task short and simple so that the monkey doesn't have to think too much about it, and watch your colleagues as they slowly start questioning just what you did to get so much attention.

Assign Roles, Not Tasks
One interesting piece of research that has come from our kindergartens and into the corporate jungle is that people are more willing to contribute when they are assigned a role, rather than a task.

The science shows that when you reward or praise someone for being a good *something*–be it a secretary, project manager or CEO–they take the role to heart more significantly than if they were told that they were good at doing the task associated with that role. For instance, it's more effective to tell someone that they're a good negotiator than to say that they did a good job in the negotiation. Praise the team member's role to generate enthusiasm and enjoy better results.

How To Get Anything You Want

If you've got any chronic naysayers in your office, try using some of the most common sales solutions from the automotive industry.

Solution Selling is the practice of asking information-seeking questions until you find out what problem the other person is dealing with, then phrase your offer accordingly. In the jungle this would look something like, "I know you're really frustrated with this group, but if you join this committee you'll be able to get the results that you need for your project."

Provocation-based selling comes right out and addresses the problem or underlying angst the other person is experiencing. One proactive way to get more work out of an obstinate monkey could be to say, "Gosh, I hear they are getting ready for another round of cuts. Do you want to work on this project with me to build out your resume? Couldn't hurt!"

Strip-lining involves agreeing with others in a way that makes them feel insecure about their decisions. This is often used to increase sales for luxury products and the imbedded sense of disapproval can immediately spark a monkey's ego and move him into action. The simple words "you know, this is *probably* good enough. I think you should go for it." can easily open up a conversation on how to improve.

Get Your Foot in the Door

If your monkeys are apprehensive of big changes but seem amenable to small ones, try the foot-in-the-door technique, in which you ask for small favors or small amounts of resources, then repeatedly talk about how much of an impact they've made, and increase the size of your request over time.

For example, when you need an hour with the CEO to discuss the direction of your project, start by asking for 15 minutes and making those 15 minutes the most efficient and rewarding meeting your boss has ever been in. Once she associates the small amounts of time or resources spent on you with positive outcomes, she'll be much more inclined to give you more attention the next time you ask.

Get Them to Slam the Door

Depending on how adventurous your manager is, you may be able to use the door-in-the-face technique, which involves over-stating your terms and then graciously settling for something less, i.e. the thing you wanted in the first place.

While this is really the most impactful method overall, you need to gauge the office environment carefully before undertaking it, especially if you are new there. In some situations you'll want to win the trust of key players before making big requests so that you don't come off as demanding, while in other situations your boldness may be interpreted as a sign of strength and willingness to make big changes.

Get What You Want Out of Meetings

We've already discussed a number of ways to get the best results out of your meetings: sitting in the right position, assuming the right posture and saying the right things. There is, however, one slightly sneaky way to get everyone in the meeting to agree with you, and it can be particularly useful when you're dealing with a tough or indecisive crowd.

When people are tired and have low blood sugar they have less self-control and will be more inclined to fire off answers in order to get out of meetings and on to their next meal. This makes midday (pre-lunch) or end-of-day meetings particularly effective if the goal for the meeting is to come to a consensus.

On the other hand, it's not effective when you need people to be on their A game, for which the best time is mid-morning. If you need to have a productive afternoon meeting, suggest holding it in another building, particularly if getting to that destination requires the staff to go outside to reach that spot. The combination of light exercise, fresh air and natural light will reset everyone's afternoon energy and make that meeting as productive as a morning meeting.

Limit Their Options

Another way to steer the outcome of your meetings is to limit the options you make available. In one study, people who were given a large variety of samples were only 10% as likely to purchase the samples as those who were given a limited number of options to choose from. So unless you're hosting an open-ended brainstorming session, make sure that you present just a few good options to harness the energy of the group and get them to focus.

You can further influence the group's decision by how you word the different parts of the agenda, and where you place them. Items that appear toward the top of the page are generally considered more valuable. Combine that with the use of powerful words such as "start" and "success" and pepper your less favorite options with less powerful words like "challenge" and "downside" so meeting participants will have no other option but to follow your lead.

How to Get What You're Worth

Many people feel as though they are overlooked for promotions and special assignments, but few of them are aware that their bosses aren't actively looking for someone to move up the ladder. The real key to getting attention and a promotion is quite simple: you have to ask for it.

We make the mistake of expecting people to recognize our innate talents and accomplishments and celebrate them, while forgetting that they have their own lives–and in the case of managers, the lives of many other employees–on their minds. The only way to overcome this challenge is to put in the legwork to promote ourselves to our bosses and ask for what we need, and to many of us, this is the most intimidating thing you could ask them to do at work.

Well, ladies, today is the day that you're going to stop being intimidated! If you need something, you're going to make a plan as to why you deserve it, convince yourself of it, do some power poses, and then head into the office to ask for that thing (whether it be a raise, more staffers, or access to information). In most cases, there are more resources available, and the real secret to snagging them is knowing how to ask for them.

Monkeys are natural investors, and will want to see some return for their bananas. If you walk into a monkey's office saying that you've been working really hard and that's why you deserve a raise, your boss may think, "But I pay you to work hard!" On the other hand, if you approach the situation as a value proposition and show that these resources will enable you to do even greater things than what you've already accomplished, the monkey will be much more apt to listen.

One key element in getting what you want is convincing yourself, in the very bottom of your soul, that you are worth it. A corporate trainer taught me to make a big, fat list of the amazing things you've done and convince yourself that you're worth double what you're about to request. That way there won't be an ounce of doubt in your expression when you march into your boss's office, and you'll be so confident in asking for a normal-sized raise that this monkey will have no way to refuse you. Remember, confidence and appearances are everything in the jungle.

Recap: Practice Black Magic

Don't Think of It as a Trick
Too many people make the mistake of thinking of black magic as a set of tricks. It's not. It's simply a skill set that allows you to communicate your needs and desires with people on a subconscious level, designed by Mother Nature herself.

Arrange Your Office for Power
Power has more to do with perception than anything else, so make sure that your body language, clothes and surroundings support this idea. Arrange your furniture in a way that draws attention to you while establishing boundaries, and use lighting and furniture that make you appear more powerful, like higher chairs and well-placed lights.

Program Others to Think Highly of You
Subtly mention previous accomplishments and link your name to important subject matter, making it impossible not to think of successful campaigns and your truly in the same sentence. When you first meet someone, tell a story about a previous experience and refer to yourself by name in the third person to sear your name into their memory.

Sell Your Ideas
Engage people's natural inclinations and fears in order to sell your ideas, get additional funding and support and get people to pay attention.

Use Senses and Instincts to Get Ahead

Remember that you're an animal and that you're working with a bunch of animals. All of us are designed by evolution to respond to certain triggers: food, sex, light, color, danger and excitement. Always keep this in mind when planning your office strategy.

Condition Others for Your Success

There are no mammals that don't enjoy a pleasant experience. Make sure that every experience others have with you is positive by using the right energy, saving affection for the right moment and making your office an addictive place so that others will offer information, loyalty and assistance in order to enter. Always keep chocolate in your desk.

Meet: The Queen of the Jungle

Now that you've mastered the tools you'll need to go from surviving to thriving in the corporate jungle, you may ask yourself: "what does thriving actually look like?"

On a fundamental level, it means that you can approach your professional life with confidence and focus, both of which will accelerate your career. You can spend your energy setting up situations to be successful, rather than doing damage control. And most importantly, you will be an empowered, aware and active creator of your professional life.

From the outside, your peers and supervisors will see you as more engaged, present and assertive, and while some people may be thrown by your greater focus on work, they will eventually come to respect you for being reliable and predictable. People will spend less time sharing gossip with you, and instead your bosses will start noticing you and entrusting you with meeting company goals. If all goes well, you'll quickly find yourself evolving from worker ant to queen bee.

Being empowerment also means that you can choose how many of these tools to use. For some of you, going in as a full-fledged alpha might transform your career beyond your wildest dreams. For others, you may realize that being a full-time alpha is nothing short of exhausting, or that it just doesn't work for you or your office.

Take my current workplace, for instance. Working at a university does not lend itself or necessitate me to be assertive and strategic to get my job done, and in many ways actually requires me to tap into my more nurturing side to guide my students–many of who are millennials and are not used to receiving feedback from alphas–through their first professional experiences. So instead of being a full-fledged alpha, I apply the tools in this book on an as-needed basis.

One way that I use the tools is that I make sure to act in a way that conveys my authority to my students, as millennials are often overly comfortable with superiors and get into hot water for misjudging boundaries. I communicate in a style more befitting an alpha so that the students can experience different forms of feedback before wandering out into the corporate jungle. That way they learn to respect authority, while also internalizing that feedback is not personal. We are all here to work!

Above all, knowing the things I talk about in this book has helped me reframe my own experiences in the corporate jungle, which consisted of equal amounts of glorious victories, productive spans and periods where everything seemed to be going wrong. Because I internalized my failures and failed to celebrate my victories, I always felt as though I had a Scarlet Letter pinned to my chest. After reexamining my past I was able to see how my well-intended actions were misinterpreted, and where I failed to recognize budding problems and take other people's paradigms into consideration. I also realized that above all, I had always done a great job, and that my rubbing my colleagues the wrong way was their problem, not mine.

These realizations have allowed me to look back at my tougher experiences in the corporate jungle with understanding and compassion–both towards others and myself–and to become friends with the monkeys. Whenever I enter a new and strange environment, I am able to quickly assess people's goals and priorities, their passions and their pains, and work with them in a meaningful way, rather than waste time trying to do things the old way. Who would have known that acting more like a beast and less than a human could lead to so much success in the corporate jungle?

No matter what your version of thriving looks like, I hope that the information in this book helps you find your place in the corporate jungle, your roar, and a new appreciation for office politics.

About the Author

Jennifer Thomé is an author who writes about psychology, health, communications and culture, as well as China, and when required to, military technology. She is a Jane of all Trades, and a professional corporate jungle guide who can talk to monkeys and humans in all necks of the jungle.

While working as a journalist, she noticed that professional women were often hesitant to be interviewed for articles or to speak candidly about the ongoing inequalities of the workplace. Curious about whether or not there was an epidemic of "impostor syndrome" among female professionals, Jennifer started researching the hidden social dynamics of the workplace, leading to the creation of *Don't Smile at the Monkeys*. This book is the culmination of years of interviews and research into animal behavior, biology and corporate psychology, coupled with her own experiences working in both corporate and government organizations.